GLOBAL CITY BLUES

GLOBAL CITY

DANIEL SOLOMON

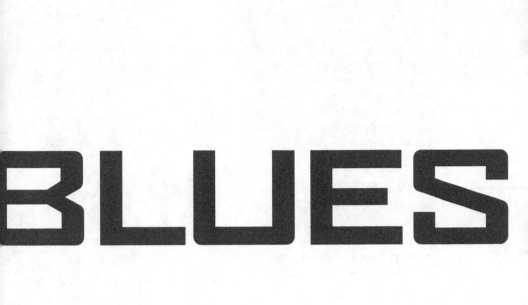

BLUES

LAND PRESS · WASHINGTON · COVELO · LONDON

ISLAND PRESS is a trademark of
The Center for Resource Economics.

Images 1 and 3 reprinted with permission from
Eichler Homes: Design for Living, by Jerry Ditto
© 1995. Photographs by Marvin Wax. Published
by Chronicle Books, LLC. San Francisco. Visit
http://www.chroniclebooks.com.

Image 2 reprinted with permission from
Julius Shulman.

Images 5.1, 5.2, and 5.3 © Landesbildstelle Berlin.

Image 23 reprinted with permission from Walter
Gropius, *The New Architecture and the Bauhaus.*
Published by MIT Press.

Library of Congress Cataloging-in-Publication data.
Solomon, Daniel, 1939–
   Global city blues / by Daniel Solomon.
     p. cm.
Includes bibliographical references and index.
   ISBN 1-55963-184-8 (alk. paper)
  1. City planning. 2. Urbanization. 3. Architecture
and society. 4. Modernism (Aesthetics) I. Title.
   NA9095.S64 2003
   720′.9173′2—dc21

                    2003001908

British Cataloguing-in-Publication data available.

Book design by Tsang Seymour Design

Composition by Wilsted & Taylor
Publishing Services

Printed on recycled, acid-free paper ✪

Manufactured in the United States of America
10 9 8 7 6 5 4 3 2 1

FOR SHIRLEY AND GEORGE

Contents

Introduction

The technologies of the last century—the automobile, the air conditioner, television, and the computer—have each in different ways transformed human settlements, habitation, and work. In just the last fifty years, we have invented ways of living that alter our experience fundamentally. We replace direct and spontaneous interactions among people with indirect and selective ones. We build in ways that sever us from weather, seasons, and the passage of time. We obliterate the distinctiveness of places and create new forms of geographic confusion.

For a long time, many have embraced these and all other forms of modernity as the inevitable workings of history. For more than fifty years, people trained in architecture, town planning, or branches of civil engineering that are part of town building were drugged with a sneaky form of Hegelian dialectics. Through our schooling and through the writings of a cadre of theorists, practitioners, and critics, a whole generation of architects and planners came to believe that we were the agents of history, bringing to an awaiting world the good news of the inevitable. The inevitable included the dominance of the private automobile and the infrastructure and town forms that support it. More recently, it has come to include much more—the globalization of the world economy and of world culture, from architecture to music to food.

This ethos of modernity has dominated city building and architecture worldwide for half a century. For many people, many architects among them, modernist aesthetics are as compelling at the beginning of the twenty-first century as they were in the middle of the twentieth century. There is no denying the seductiveness of the spatial complexities, the technological materials, the inventiveness and the dazzle of the best modern buildings. Modern architecture brought with it, however, an ideology about city planning that should by now be as thoroughly discredited by fifty calamitous years of city building as any ideas in history. Such is not the case, however, and much contention and confusion remains. Disentangling architectural invention and enjoyment of new technologies from the dogmas and practices of modernist city planning has proved to be a complicated matter.

While modernity and modernist town planning in its various forms have come to dominate the world, some have fled the hegemony of the global city, have fought it, or have created new tribalisms, sometimes violent or crazy ones, bent on the recapture of some earlier time, real or imagined, that was spiritually more congenial. The rage of Mohammed Atta, the gentle-appearing young man who, on September 11, 2001, piloted American Airlines Flight 11 into the World Trade Center, was, as far as we know, at least partially a reaction to his training and experience as a town planner and his close view of world tourism's assault on ancient agrarian villages of the Nile.

One does not have to be a terrorist capable of monstrous acts to feel a deep sense of something terribly amiss with many new places we see being built. We know instinctively that something is wrong with a whole series of daily experiences that have become commonplace in towns and parts of towns we have built in the last fifty years but that were not everyday occurrences before then. We know that something is wrong when our desk is seventy-five feet from a window that doesn't open and that transmits only 15 percent of the light of the day. We know that something is wrong when every day at lunch, everybody looks like us, is the same age, and does the same kind of work. We know that something is wrong with tasteless food that comes from the steam table. Streets with no people on them, and places where we rarely see people poorer or richer or older than ourselves, are somehow troubling.

On our vacations, we go to where the food tastes better, to places where people who are interesting to look at gather in cafés, and where we can walk around and do things. Except for compulsive gamblers, most of us never spend our discretionary time in places where you cannot tell the time of day. Primates in the social environment of monkey island at the zoo look like they are doing all right, jumping around outside with their friends. But primates isolated in cages in research labs look terrible; you can see the sadness and desperation in their eyes. We are no different; when our environment does not suit our genetic makeup, bad things happen to our health and our spirits.

This is a book about the making of cities and the buildings that compose them. It is about the conditions under which an architect engaged in those activities now works, how those conditions evolved, and why they are changing. It is about the qualities of life threatened by the ways cities are built at the beginning of the twenty-first century, and it is about intelligent response to those threats. It is about why the city planning ideas and the cultural Cuisinart that came in the box with modern architecture are a lingering menace.

As a foot soldier in the making of the world, an architect has a particularly grubby and intimate view of what is happening to the way we live. In his daily routine, he may not confront the grand strategies of macroeconomics, but each day the architect plunges into a nether world of codes, laws, technologies, products, business practices, and ideologies, tacit and overt, that shape the common experience of almost everyone on earth. Like a sausage maker or a gynecologist, an architect cannot help knowing more than most people want to know about certain subjects. This book is written in the hope that an architect's view from the foxhole can contribute to the quest to keep the qualities of our lives from being eternally diminished by all the things and procedures that human beings invent so cleverly and relentlessly.

Global City Blues accepts the inevitability of technological change with neither celebration nor despair. It is in part about the dogged and occasionally successful struggle of many to work in the conditions of the present to create places that satisfy the deepest longings that people have for the places they live. This struggle is by no means the first reform movement directed at architecture and town planning in the last two hundred years of rapid technological change, population growth, and urbanization. But unlike earlier reform movements, this one is directed at particular conditions and threats presented by the dominant economics and technologies at the beginning of the twenty-first century. It involves the efforts of all sorts of people, from farmers, grocers, and cooks to politicians and bureaucrats. Architects and town planners have their own role in all this—and not a small one.

The book contains reflections about the movement called New Urbanism, which several colleagues and I helped launch a decade ago and of which we continue to be a part. Its proponents see New Urbanism as a broad, embracing set of ideas about the future of our cities and city-regions, as a reversal of some aspects of orthodox modern architecture, but more particularly of modernist town planning.

The planning ideologies that so radically altered the man-made world after World War II were born of a unique historical moment that bred forms of hubris, optimism, and contempt for the past that the world had never seen before. In many arenas, the failure of those ideas and the prescriptions that emanated from them are clear, and have been clear for a long time. There are no remaining apologists for the American urban renewal, public housing, and urban highway programs of the 1950s and 1960s. And though, in some settings, the marketplace still seems to support suburban sprawl and the decanting of life from older urban centers, dissatisfaction with those building conventions is also widespread, growing, and passionate. Nonetheless, the juggernaut of auto-dominated global suburbia rolls on.

New Urbanism is a broadly formulated alternative, intended to redirect town building so that the common experience of people is richer than the soul-numbing environments of business parks, freeway commuting, and walled residential enclaves where everybody is the same age, color, and tax bracket. New Urbanism is a synthesis of ideas that have been brewing in the minds of urban critics, environmentalists, and some architectural thinkers since the 1960s. It clarifies the inherent linkages between the policies that have produced the catastrophe of suburban sprawl and the abandonment of older urban centers. It argues for a re-constitution of architecture's traditional and essential role in shaping the public space of towns. The policies and specific prescriptions of New Urbanism have been addressed in other settings and other books. *Global City Blues* is about why those policies and prescriptions are elements of something that is so very important. In many of its manifestations, the global city is a fundamental assault on simple pleasures, appetites, and needs that are part of our biology. New Urbanism belongs to a healthy, necessary culture of resistance to that assault.

The book is a series of linked essays, some of which were written at different times. Each is independent, but together they examine and develop recurrent themes. They follow the path from my own indoctrination into the set of beliefs that gave shape to cities, towns, and our life experience after World War II to the evolution of a new set of beliefs born of reaction to that experience and confrontation with what lies ahead.

GLOBAL CITY BLUES

PART 1

NEARNESS

In the evolutionary history of humans, the period of modernist town planning and the technologies that support it are not even a blip on the chart. The genetic codes that direct our most basic impulses were written long, long ago by our Paleolithic and Neolithic ancestors, whose survival depended upon their sociability and the subtlety of their understanding of the world around them, first as hunter/gatherers and later as farmers but always in defense against their enemies. In a few short years, we cannot simply erase the physical and cognitive tracks along which we have traveled with brilliant biological success for scores of millennia. Our species succeeds because we are alert, observant, and sociable creatures; a major part of what we demand from our habitat is regular exercise of these fundamental parts of our humanity.

In many ways, our recent patterns of making buildings and towns tend to deny us this life-sustaining exercise, and we now routinely experience the condition that philosopher Martin Heidegger referred to as "loss of nearness." The central concept of Heidegger's writings—"being in the world"—establishes a fundamental relationship between our consciousness and the context of our lives. It is from this relationship that the idea of nearness emerged. He considered its loss to be a deep spiritual and cultural malaise that infiltrates experience at almost every moment of our lives.

The first task in addressing this malaise is to recognize its occurrence—to know when some aspect of the way we are living interferes with our preferred ways of interacting with other people and the world around us. When we achieve this recognition, the physical design of buildings, towns, and the ways we move about takes on a new significance. With this recognition, we become part of a collective struggle to reconfigure our daily world so that it is more like the places we seek out when we have the chance, and less like the places that we know deep in our genes do not satisfy everything we long for. This struggle is to construct a world of "nearness" in all its dimensions when, for many complex reasons, it is no longer easy to do so.

The four essays of Part 1 describe the experience of nearness in daily life and its several common antonyms: the indirect, the indistinct, the virtual, and the isolating. They provide a framework for what recent reforms in town planning and architecture hope to achieve and what they must overcome.

Measure the Night with Bells

Imagine a raging river that spills over its banks and tears through lowlands dotted with oaks. Large trees that become uprooted add to the water's rage and sweep smaller objects with them. The larger and more magnificent the uprooted tree, the more damage it does. Some large trees remain rooted, and they slow the torrent and make their own little dams from the detritus swept along by the flood. If you think of the cascade of events of the last half century as a flood, then one could say that the stoutest and most firmly rooted oak tree, the one that has stood the longest and resisted the swirling torrent where it is most furious, is Professor Wu Liangyong, former director of the School of Architecture and Urban Planning at Tsinghua University in Beijing.

Over the course of his long life, Professor Wu has witnessed the displacement of feudalism by Republican China, the Japanese occupation, the Communist Revolution, and later the terrible upheavals of the Cultural Revolution. He saw the rebirth of Chinese mercantilism—slow at first, but accelerating like a rocket—and he saw the disintegration of the bamboo curtain, and then the massive arrival of global capitalism and world tourism. He saw most of the graceful city of his childhood destroyed, stone by stone. He saw what was built in the name of socialism following Soviet models, and he has seen later generations of construction that look more like Las Vegas, in which the linkage to socialism is much harder to discern. He has seen the population of his city quadruple, and he has witnessed the transition from a populace that moved about almost exclusively by bicycle, silently, to one that drives millions of cars and trucks every day.

Through all of this, Professor Wu has been one of the very few who have systematically preserved the record of the dismantled city and the memory of its beauty. He is the most important architect to attempt to adapt that ancient grace to the torrents of change that have swirled around him all of his life. His Ju'er Hutong is the only major housing project of recent vintage in Beijing that attempts to address new conditions based on an understanding and love for Beijing's magnificent heritage of courtyard housing. The Ju'er Hutong has the light, air, and living accommodation of modern housing, the density demanded by modern development pressure, and all the civic virtues of traditional courtyard housing. Given the tumult he has lived through, Professor Wu could not fail to understand that radical upheavals are inevitable, but he has resolutely refused to accept the idea that change necessarily carries with it the eradication of history and the diminution of the pleasures of city life. Now, in his eighties, bright-eyed and intensely active, many others have begun to see what his lonely, stubborn, resourceful quest has been about, and that a contradiction does not necessarily exist between rootedness and the embrace of change.

The spirit that roots Professor Wu, that endows him with his quiet serenity and his recent influence, is the inverse of the spirit that has been celebrated, lionized, and rewarded in the hermetic, self-perpetuating culture of the architectural world for most of the last seventy-five years.

If Wu Liangyong is the embodiment of a rooted tree, then consider the case of a very large uprooted tree, one that crashes through all sorts of things that the waters alone would not have swept away. Dutch architect Rem Koolhaas is what one might call an uprooted tree of just this sort. In the year 2000, the architectural profession marked the turning of the millennium by awarding Koolhaas its highest honor, the Pritzker Prize. The millennial new year was a moment for large-scale pyrotechnics around the world, the celebrating of new beginnings and the severing of old ways. There were good reasons for the 2000 Pritzker selection, for Rem Koolhaas is the champion of new beginnings and probably the world's most provocative apologist for new forms of the human condition.

People interested in town planning and architecture should be aware, however, that their own man of that special hour has some odd preferences, in addition to his obvious gifts. The Pritzker laureate at the dawn of the millennium is also the poet laureate of airline food, endless shopping malls, and the new Chinese cities where thousands of identical high-rises are built from the same brief, simple, and rapidly produced set of computer drawings. He embraces foul air, adores porn shops, and laments their disappearance from Times Square. What constitutes dystopia for most are kinky thrills for the 2000 Pritzker winner. He celebrates an image of schoolgirls strolling past a bloated corpse in Lagos as part of "a paradigmatic case study of a city at the forefront of globalizing modernity." He considers himself one of philosopher Peter Sloterdijl's "kinetic elite," those who live in airports, places "with the added attraction of being hermetic systems from which there is no escape—except to another airport." What is good in the world, he recently announced, "is not a category that interests me."

The Pritzker jury did their part to launch the next chapter of the human story from a new confluence of high culture, consumer capitalism, and nihilist chic. Perhaps this should only be troubling to people who choose to be troubled by it. Most of us don't like global warming, do like good food, consider fresh air to be salutary, and—philistine though it may be—take pleasure in the places we live. We can say that Koolhaas engages us by shocking us, in the way that blood-soaked punk bands or Benneton ads with AIDS patients engage us—as audacious, half-ironic manipulations of media culture. We can feel free to ignore it all and go unfretfully about our sane little lives, away from the cutting edge.

But Koolhaas is a student of another polemical architect from modernity's original incarnation, that other brilliant writer and media maven *par excellence*, Le Corbusier, whose influence was not exactly negligible. Koolhaas's way of being in the world, of shocking, of anticipating the new, of resisting convention, his very conception of the space of the city, are appropriated from Le Corbusier. This should be a little unnerving, because we might not now be tearing down whole districts of uninhabitable public housing towers or struggling to find the money to remove the elevated highways that tore our cities apart if Le Corbusier had not so completely seduced an earlier generation of architectural teachers and students, just as Koolhaas has done. Le Corbusier's polemical exhibitions of the 1920s, *The City for Three Million* and *Radiant City,* and his book *Towards a New Architecture* became sacred images and texts for young architects. Le Corbusier's wit, the acerbic brilliance of his writing, and the beauty of the images he produced convinced an entire generation that the urban culture of the world had had it, that it was obsolete, irrelevant, and inappropriate for a new kind of human, who was the unique product of the twentieth century.

Some historians now downplay the influence of Le Corbusier and point to others in the 1920s and 1930s who built more and had similar ideas. But it is impossible to claim that the polemic of his Radiant City did not change the world. Radiant City's widely spaced "Cartesian" high-rises, standing in a verdant park, bisected by giant motorways came to pass, not always just as Le Corbusier intended, but they came to pass massively and all over the world. At this point, it is hard to find anyone willing to argue that this has been a beneficent experience for all of us.

It is a crucial part of the story of the modernist city that Le Corbusier chose the term "Cartesian" to describe the skyscrapers of his imagination. What he meant by the evocation of Descartes was that these buildings would be the perfect embodiment of rational thought, standing free and unfettered in a matrix of undifferentiated space. They would ignore and ultimately eradicate the messy, irrational layering of centuries that burdened cities and distorted their architecture. It is striking how banal his utopian skyscraper of 1935 sounds today:

> *Surfaced with solemn marble, shining with clear mirrors mounted in stainless steel frames. Silence. Corridors and vast spaces; doors open automatically: they are the silent elevators unloading passengers. No windows anywhere. . . . Silent walls. "Conditioned" air throughout, pure, clean, at a constant temperature. Am I on the fifth floor or the fortieth?*

Le Corbusier's pungent prose, his fascination with new experiences that are astonishing but otherwise uninteresting, sounds just like the latest and hippest polemic from Rem Koolhaas. It is tempting to think that Koolhaas is a bright, charming, harmless fellow, harmless because he is a cult figure principally just to architecture students and their young teachers. But good God, look what the architecture students and young teachers of Le Corbusier's day did to the world the minute they got the chance. They actually constructed the *tabula rasa* of Cartesian space that Le Corbusier imagined. In America, they wrought the generation of slum clearance and urban renewal, isolated "rational" buildings in a matrix of undifferentiated space that left inner cities decimated; they built elevated highways that wrecked urban neighborhoods and waterfronts. They planned and built the calamitous public housing towers of Chicago, the South Bronx, and Pruitt-Igo in St. Louis (so disastrous that it was blown up on national television in 1972). In England, a generation of Corbu acolytes produced the New Brutalist movement of the 1950s and 1960s, and the now-aging concrete relics of that period form large, long-lasting scars on the lovely face of London. The grim, utterly depressing outskirts of St. Petersburg, which look so much like Le Corbusier schemes from the 1920s, are what happened when the dogmas of modernist town planning displaced classical training for architects in the Soviet Union after Stalin's death in 1953. Today in Beijing, one can drive down a motorway lined with freestanding high-rises, and it is *exactly* as if one is inside a Le Corbusier sketch. Maybe it all would have happened anyway, but not with the vigor, the conviction, the sense of rectitude that Le Corbusier gave to the drift of history. Recently in Brussels, Glasgow, St. Louis, Chicago, and San Francisco, people have gleefully blown the remnants of Radiant City to smithereens, but in the *arriviste* economies of China and Southeast Asia they are building it by the mile as if the year were 1952 and Radiant City could still wear its mantle of untested innocence.

Le Corbusier's genius was that he saw the relationship among three things: a stick, a brightly colored piece of cloth, and a runaway train. He called the brightly colored piece of cloth a flag, he called the stick a flagpole, and he leapt onto the runaway train with the pole and flag and called the train a revolution. He declared that the terrified people trapped in the train were heroes of the revolution. When they heard this, the experience of not being able to control the direction or speed of the train was transformed from terror to that of a thrill ride. Koolhaas is a similar champion of the remorseless charge of modernity, the runaway train he sees as an uncontrollable force.

But madness begets madness. The madness of hypermodernism begets the countermadness of Jihad: Theodore Kaczynski and Timothy

McVeigh at home, Slobodan Milosevic, Islamic fundamentalism, and the extremes of the Israeli right abroad. The endless wave of "globalizing modernity" that Koolhaas so cleverly and joyfully rides like a surfer is precisely what drives some others into bomb production.

Globalizing modernity has many dimensions, political, economic, and cultural, but part of what propels the phenomenon and gives it the character of inevitability is the irresistible attractiveness of certain technologies. One has to go to remote places to find anyone whose life is not fundamentally shaped by the combined effects of mankind's four most transformative technical innovations: the automobile, the air conditioner, television, and the computer.

Air conditioning is the enabling mechanism for the universal Marriotts and the shopping malls that are identical in sweltering Panama City and in freezing Stockholm. It is responsible for the atrophy of an ancient body of knowledge through which builders crafted habitation from the equator to the Arctic Circle. Air conditioning, while it makes us comfortable anywhere, obliterates the time of day, the weather, the seasons, and the distinctiveness of the places of the world.

Television was the first great threat to face-to-face contact as the principal way people understand one another. Before television it was hard to imagine a challenge to the café, the church, the street, the piazza, the concert hall, and the stadium as the loci of our shared experience.

The automobile built the city of the last half of the twentieth century. The political and economic force represented in the immortal words "What's good for General Motors is good for the country" decanted the wealth of cities, ravaged them physically and socially, and built the new world of the regional mall, the big box, the planned development, and the business park.

Because the overwhelming impact of the computer on our lives is so recent, its effects are harder to dissect and summarize than those of the other huge technologies. It is partly an emblem for new transformations, partly the technical instrument of those transformations, and like the automobile, a self-perpetuating economic force of incredible power. What is beginning to come into focus is how much the new world of hypercommunications has in common with the three other technologies—how, like the others, it has the capacity to transform what was a direct and simple act into an indirect and complex one. Ten times a day we encounter the vexations of voice mail, but that is only where our new excursions into indirection begin. E-mail consumes our days in a medium that lacks both the craft of the written word and the nuances and intimacy of the spoken word. Only the most dedicated technophiles will claim that the decade and a half that we have all spent staring at our computer screens has enriched us spiritually, has brought us closer to others, or has been a sensual pleasure in its own right.

These technologies, the ways they interact with one another, and the town planning and architecture that emanate from them constitute the condition that Martin Heidegger named "loss of nearness." Recently there was a raging controversy in San Francisco between "nearness" and its opposite that illustrates what Heidegger must have had in mind. Chinese merchants operate a highly successful street market on Stockton Street, a place also frequented by tourists. There were those who were offended by the fact that animals, mostly chickens and ducks, are kept in cages along the street and then slaughtered in public view. They apparently had difficulty accepting the idea that the ontology of chicken parts has more to it than Styrofoam trays clad in Cling Wrap. To people whose only contact with food production is the supermarket, the sight of caged animals, slaughter, and butchery was absolutely revolting. The Chinese poultry merchants, in turn, were completely bewildered. How could anyone dispute that chicken parts do come from living creatures that one must kill if one is to eat them? Fresh killed chickens are healthier and far better tasting than packaged ones that have been dead for who knows how long. The sensibility that has difficulty with these facts was reared on several modern technologies working in concert: refrigeration, inert synthetic packaging materials, and, most of all, the automobile, the birth parent of the supermarket. Uncritical champions of modernity regard these technologies as irresistible, if not beneficent. Their views do not account for the ever larger crowds of shoppers on Stockton Street and the fact that a broad segment of people have discovered that Chinatown chickens taste better, cost less, and don't make you sick. They also like shopping on a crowded street where people of all ages and incomes speak many languages.

Another example: In Houston, everything is air-conditioned—

offices, houses, gyms, cars, everything. Friends in Houston recently moved from a large air-conditioned house to an apartment in a high-rise that, surprisingly, has operable windows. Contrary to common perception, the weather in Houston is not *always* miserable. My friends discovered the pleasure (novel in Houston) of sleeping with open windows. Pretty soon they each began to have a rash of ailments: colds, allergies, aches and pains of various sorts. Their physician, after he learned about the open windows, guessed that their immune systems, after a lifetime in sealed buildings, could not handle whatever is in fresh air, at least in Houston's version of fresh air. He suggested that they sleep with the windows shut. The ailments all promptly went away. Both the environment they live in and their own physiology are so altered by the way that Houston is built that they could not indulge the unquenchable, genetically hard-wired human desire to open a window on a balmy night.

For many, global Houston or the global supermarket is no laughing matter. Panic, hatred, xenophobia, rage, psychosis, and terrorism are some of the ways that people have reacted to the "loss of nearness." Benjamin R. Barber's *Jihad vs. MacWorld* and Thomas L. Friedman's *The Lexus and the Olive Tree* convincingly present the dialectical relationship between new fundamentalisms of all sorts and the onslaught of "globalizing modernity" as celebrated by Rem Koolhaas. For Barber, it is the "inadvertent despotism" of the global mall that spawns the madness of Jihad. *Global City Blues* is intended as a counterpolemic to both forms of madness, with some sympathy for both. Being crazy, after all, is just a way of looking at things, and one can often learn something from the rantings of crazy people.

The phrase "globalizing modernity" has a sinister ring, as if there is some inexorable historical force that couples the two words and perpetuates their coupling into an ever more universal onslaught of cultural and technological homogenization. It is as if the spirit and the actual formal devices of the modernity that was conceived in Germany, Holland, and France in the 1920s and which achieved a kind of hegemony in most industrial nations immediately after World War II are projected into a future in which they displace all other forms of the human condition, past, present, and future.

There is, however, another quite opposite way of understanding the promise of globalization. Heidegger spent a significant portion of his opus *Being and Time* dismantling the narrow and impoverished Cartesian view of the world, a view that in Heideggerian terms "unworlds the world" and tries to drain things of all the meaning they have for us. For Heidegger, full-fledged space consists not of the arid universe of the x, y, and z Cartesian coordinates with disembodied objects floating around among them, but of *places* of myth and history, where people *belong* and *dwell,* and where things *matter,* because they are laden with meaning.

It is significant that at the end of the year 2001, the municipal administration of Beijing announced that, in conjunction with the Beijing Olympics of 2008, an ancient practice that had been suspended since 1924 would be reinstated. All over the city, at two-hour intervals through the night, the passage of time will be marked by the sounding of bells and the beating of drums on new towers, such as the one Professor Wu designed for the Ju'er Hutong. In addition, after more than fifty years of remorse-less destruction of the historic city in the name of progress, twenty two new historic preservation districts will be established. The scholarship of Professor Wu's fine book *Rehabilitating the Old City of Beijing* has at last found the official audience to which his lifelong quest has been directed. Finally, 1.8 kilometers of the magnificent medieval walls of Beijing will be reconstructed, salvaging wherever possible the original bricks and stones from whatever use to which they had been put. The destruction of the walls of Beijing began at the conclusion of the revolution in 1949 and was completed during the Cultural Revolution in the 1970s. The political ideas that motivated this demolition have a particularly Chinese cast, but the dates during which it occurred exactly mirror the high period of mod-ernist city planning in the United States and Western Europe.

Nothing represents the force of globalization more vividly than the Olympic Games. Yet it is the occasion of the Olympics, and the prospect of twenty-first-century world tourism descending massively on Beijing, that has finally deflected the Chinese from a half century of systematic de-struction of their own heritage. For sound reasons related to the very nature of globalization, the linkage of the words "globalizing" and "mo-dernity" is anything but inevitable, if what one means by modernity is perpetuating the dreams of the 1920s and the postwar banalities that emanated from them. If and when these new Chinese initiatives occur, people from all the world will have a good, new purpose for a trip to Beijing. They can go to inhabit a Heideggerian place, not Cartesian space. They can look forward not to a visit to a shopping mall that looks like the Denver airport but to the measuring of the night by bells, and the actual relocation of a great city in its antiquity. Perhaps it is Professor Wu Liangyong, and not Rem Koolhaas, the rooted tree and not the uprooted tree, who will be remembered as the true prophet of globalization.

Peaches

Every reformation has a counterreformation, as Karl Marx, among others, has noted. As sizable and powerful groups of people have come together under the banners of New Urbanism and Smart Growth to campaign against the decanting of life from American cities, against placeless universalism in architecture, and against the pillage of countryside by sprawl, the forces that have caused these phenomena have not exactly been dormant. Sprawl, urban disintegration, and placelessness, we discover, have their own advocates, apologists, and enthusiasts. They, too, have organizations, newsletters, circles of friends and supporters, polemical tracts, and useful political connections. All of this is part of something larger, a fundamental conflict about the nature of the world.

One way to make the nature of this conflict clear is to talk about how it manifests itself in the culture of food, which has many parallels to urbanism. Long before, maybe ten years before, there was much serious collective talk about how to reform the ways that American cities are built, there was a concerted and astonishingly successful movement to change the ways Americans cook and eat. The idea that the American diet could be nutritious, fresh, imaginative, and at the same time rooted in local traditions and crops was a revolutionary concept put forward by just a few people. Architects and urbanists frequently look with envy to the foodies for their huge cultural accomplishment. They have not only created a new American cuisine of amazing quality, but they have had an impact on the supermarket, where decent produce and tasty, nutritious products are much less of a rarity than they used to be. Even fast food has not been totally immune to the influence of the foodies.

But not so fast. While everything from haute cuisine to hamburgers has been stirred up, the food counterreformation is also well under way. Consider the career of syndicated "food writer" Carolyn Wyman, author of *Spam, a Biography: The Amazing True Story of America's "Miracle Meat."* Ms. Wyman's rhapsodic writings include recipes for such delicacies as Spam with baked beans and canned pineapple and Spam with cornflakes and condensed cream of mushroom soup. She loves Spam, Cheez Whiz, Miracle Whip—all the staples that would look just right in the kitchen of one of Rem Koolhaas's ultrachic 1950s revival houses. Carolyn Wyman and Rem Koolhaas, in their separate ways, are up to similar sorts of cultural mischief.

There is, of course, something perverse and ironic in all this. Famous architect husband and wife Robert Venturi and Denise Scott Brown, who have made ironic reference into a lifework, used to play a game together that they called "I-can-like-something-uglier-than-you-can-like." It's hard to believe that the Carolyn Wymans of the world really eat Spam; it's just that they find us arugula munchers so insufferable. If the hip young architects in their black unstructured jackets really liked the jagged shards of space they model so dazzlingly on their computers, they would live and work in them, but that is not the case. Architecture schools, architectural offices, and the dwellings of even moderately successful architects and planners are still in the really cool old parts of London, Rome, Paris, and New York, just as they have always been. London's Architectural Association, where the shards are sharpest, is in a beautiful Georgian building on Bedford Square, one of London's finest gems of eighteenth-century urbanity. Faculty, students, and trustees would not take kindly to the suggestion that a move to Euro-Lille would be more in keeping with what goes on in the school.

Cultural perversity among architects is not so unusual a phenomenon. Phillip Johnson has been the master practitioner of it for seventy-five years. As a young architect and teacher, I too found myself championing some truly awful things, principally because I thought they would be offensive to the (insufferable) sensibilities and pieties of my academic colleagues. In the spring of 1970, I authored an issue of the Walker Art

Center's *Design Quarterly,* entitled "Easy Come, Easy Go," as a celebration of glitz, vulgarity, and ecological mischief of the worst sort. The idea was that more of the built world should be like the lease-hold tenant improvements in shopping centers, designed to be thrown away after five years. That way the environments we live in could be as technically up-to-date as automobiles and as amusing, jazzy, and spirited as fashions. I did not think too hard about the cultural, ecological, and spiritual consequences of such a program, because I was a Bad Boy in the midst of a thoroughly understandable form of protracted adolescence. One might consider these polemics innocent, even wholesome, if they were not now so pervasive, with so many successful bad boys and girls causing such tragic, irreparable damage to cities and landscapes all around the world—like what Spam does to your arteries.

Food and urbanism are both fundamental to human experience. They are each in the midst of a similar crisis, and the crisis in each field is exacerbated by the amusing naughtiness of cultural mischief makers like Carolyn Wyman and Rem Koolhaas. Foodies worry that masses of people will go through life and never taste a peach that tastes like a peach. The people will survive somehow—it's *peachiness* that is threatened with extinction. In the contemporary world, retaining the full-blown potential of the flavor of a peach as a part of most people's normal life experience is no small matter. It involves land use policy, banking, union agreements, transportation, and distribution networks as much as it involves peach breeding, which itself is a more complex subject than ever before. In an agrarian society, where the peach trees are outside one's door, the perfect peach is a commonplace. Delivering perfect peaches to the modern metropolis is another question.

The circumstances that now face cities are just as complicated and just as novel. Architectural historian Robert Fishman has noted the parallels between a short fable by Jorge Luis Borges, entitled "Pierre Menard, Author of Don Quixote," and the quest to recover the virtues of traditional urbanism amid the complexities of contemporary life. In this tale, the protagonist, Pierre Menard, sets out to write a word-for-word replica of *Don Quixote.* He begins by attempting to replicate for himself the life experience of Cervantes but decides that this is too easy a way to go about duplicating Cervantes's prose, an insufficient act of the imagination. Instead he struggles for years to write verbatim passages of *Don Quixote* from his own experience as a modern Parisian. What were commonplace observations for Cervantes are supreme acts of critical intelligence for M. Menard.

The analogy that Fishman draws is this: A friendly, handsome, and walkable neighborhood was an ordinary occurrence in the nineteenth century, and its creation was an unconscious act. But when a place with the same qualities is built from the basis of our experience of "globalizing modernity" at the beginning of the twenty-first century, it is a different kind of activity. When its builders must overcome all the obstacles that now exist to achieving those once commonplace qualities, it too becomes a heroic act of critical intelligence, filled with meaning and importance that it never had before. Building a piece of city today, with qualities like those of traditional cities, is like Pierre Menard writing *Don Quixote*. For food, the situation is similar. The defense or reconstitution of Martin Heidegger's nearness of experience in defiance of a world circumstance bent on obliterating it is the highest form of critical act. Peachiness is a form of nearness; urbanity is another.

A revivified sense of town life, and architecture that supports it, constitutes a resistance movement. What is resisted is the quality of life that is the inadvertent by-product of modernist planning dogma added to the four transformative technologies of the twentieth century: the automobile, the air conditioner, television, and the computer. All but the air conditioner were conceived as ways to link people together, but all four have centrifugal reactions of potent force as instruments of isolation. They each are responsible for patterns of isolation of people from others, of isolation from one's sense of location in time and space, and of isolation from direct, sentient experience of the world. This resistance movement is the struggle to recover, reinforce, and reinvent the immediacy of direct experience in a world of virtual or indirect experience.

What is emphatically *not* at issue or proposed here is resistance to these technologies themselves. It is too hopeless, too dumb, even to imagine that any of the four will somehow simply go away. The movement known as New Urbanism should not be confused with various attempts to repeal the twentieth century. It is, instead, a quest to recover the immediacy of the experience of town life under the conditions imposed by the four technologies and the legacy of public policies that directed the building of cities and suburbs after World War II.

Other fields have corollary movements, including cooking, product design, agricultural preservation, wildlife conservation, and various branches of civil engineering. Bit by bit people in these fields are learning one another's codes, signals, and covert signs, a necessary step in the building of a powerful conspiracy. Those interested in the fate of cities should pay close attention to how the food revolution was conducted to learn not only about the joys of the palate but about crucial strategic and tactical lessons as well.

Alice

Alice Waters is the owner of Chez Panisse in Berkeley, which is to new American cuisine what the Vatican is to Catholicism. There is something surprising and disarming about Alice when you meet her. She doesn't seem like a famous person who caused a revolution, like Lenin or Le Corbusier. She is friendly and gentle—a pretty, vulnerable-looking woman. It is only after you know her a bit that you see under the soft manner the qualities people look for in a head of state or a middle linebacker: fearlessness, force of will, a degree of grandiosity, a determination that is almost, but not quite, demented.

I saw Alice recently at a party. I didn't know any of the guests except her, and she was in the kitchen madly washing champagne glasses, because it needed doing. We chatted while she washed and got slightly swacked on champagne laced with something like Cassis but much tastier and more alcoholic. She told me about her current project, a big project and a big source of frustration for her. She had been asked by the directors of the Louvre, no less, to create a restaurant as part of the museum. Imagine that—an American woman, from Berkeley, asked to create *the* restaurant for *the* Louvre, in Paris. For this modest-appearing woman washing the champagne glasses, this was an opportunity, *the* opportunity, to do something much more ambitious and important than just create the restaurant at the Louvre. For her, it was the chance for the cultural establishment of France to stand up against the agricultural policies of the government and some powerful sections of the European Union. In her view, the culinary traditions of France are absolutely linked to agriculture and the culture of the countryside. She believes—*passionately* believes—that French cuisine, and particularly Parisian cuisine, will be irreparably damaged by the current generation of agricultural politics and policies. The food of Paris depends on lots of little specialty crops grown right near the city, where they can be transported fresh. Pan-European macro agri-biz, with its rationalized system of subsidies, does not have much tolerance for this sort of thing.

What Alice proposed for the Louvre was both a restaurant and a polemical exhibition that would put the relationships between food and the organization of agriculture, distribution systems, and economic policy right on people's palates and thus directly in their heads. The world would surely be better to live in if there were more city planners, more architects, more politicians, and more citizens who see the relationships between public policy and the quality of daily experience that Alice sees, and she was not willing to settle for anything less than the full realization of her vision.

The experience of visitors to this polemical restaurant/museum would be like that of my Berkeley graduate students on the night that I invited two of Alice's cohorts to a seminar. They were Patricia Untermann, San Francisco restaurant owner and food writer, and Sibella Kraus, executive director of a nonprofit called Sustainable Agriculture Education (SAGE). The seminar for architecture and planning students was entitled "Regionalism," and the occasion of the invitation was a fascinating article that Patricia Untermann had written on Basque separatism, the revival of Basque cuisine, and the concurrent rediscovery of local vernacular building traditions in the Basque country.

The guests arrived at class with bags of groceries and distributed to each student two string beans, two cherry tomatoes, two peppers, two plums, two apricots, and two little bunches of table grapes. One of each pair of items came from the supermarket; the other, from the group of farmers and purveyors that Sibella Kraus had helped organize to supply Chez Panisse, some other Bay Area restaurants, and the San Francisco Farmer's Market. The differences in the taste, colors, and aromas between each of the pairs of items were absolutely stunning.

Sibella, who seems to know more about this sort of thing than any-

one else on earth, then proceeded to describe in detail the land ownership, farming methods, biochemistry, land use policies, distribution
networks, storage methods, marketing strategies, and economics of
each piece of produce. The students (and the teacher) were spellbound,
and years later, many in that class remember the experience as a major
epiphany. What was demonstrated so memorably was the relationship
between how things are organized and what life is like, and how very
different the diminished experience of the supermarket is from what one
might think of as the real thing.

Alice Waters and her colleagues like Patricia Untermann and
Sibella Kraus are one of the major forces that have transformed American food. Another is Julia Child, but Alice Waters and Julia Child are very
different from each other. Alice believes that cooking begins with agriculture and with forage, and she is quite willing to challenge the whole
organization of *everything* to insure that our food supply supports a
cuisine that has integrity from beginning to end. Like Alice, Julia Child is
a missionary, but her mission, in part, is to bring civilization to normal
people through means that include the normal stuff from the supermarket. That is what she thinks is important, and it is significant that her chosen medium is television. Her TV recipes are usually made from ingre-
dients anyone can buy most anywhere, and she made herself into such a
TV personality that a twenty-second caricature of her voice is instantly
recognizable to the audience of *Saturday Night Live* or *Prairie Home
Companion.*

Alice Waters and Julia Child are two kinds of polemicists. One is
willing to propose the fundamental reorganization of the world; the other
does not see that as a practical proposition but thinks that the survival of
civilization depends upon our ability to function within institutions and
processes we can't control. Julia Child also worries more about what food
costs than Alice Waters does.

But it is not as if Alice is a head-in-the-sand ideologue, like those architectural polemicists who insist that the twentieth century was just a
big mistake that never should have happened and now should be ignored
or repealed. Leon Krier, Christopher Alexander, Prince Charles, and Quin-
lan Terry all, at various times, have inhabited this camp. Alice and her
half dozen hard-core cadres are tough and pragmatic politicians whose

impact on the world is largely the product of hard-won victories over formidable opposition.

Think what it took to make their Edible Schoolyard for the Berkeley Public Schools a reality. The Edible Schoolyard is a curriculum through which students prepare meals from organic produce raised on school grounds by their own labor. Think how many public agencies, how many funders, and how many neighborhood organizations had to be persuaded before San Francisco would allow a fabulous Saturday farmer's market right in the middle of town featuring the best organic everything from all over Northern California.

Julia Child would probably not take on these battles, but her impact on the American table is also huge and is the result of an extraordinary energy and a totally original way of being. The tension between Alice Waters's culinary politics and Julia Child's, and the importance of both, is a theme that recurs throughout this book. Both of these remarkable women have done good in the world. Both are models for what architects and town builders need to do. Reforming town building is such a complex and formidable undertaking that there are times when it is good to be Alice and times when it is absolutely necessary to be Julia. This distinction between these two modes of strategic behavior—remaking the world, and civilizing an unalterable world—will reappear later.

The Monster

One could say that there are vast forces at work in the world that are roughly analogous to good and evil. The evil forces are those that tend to wreck the world and turn it into an uncongenial place for its inhabitants, human and otherwise. Evil has its roots in greed, short-sightedness, and bad ideas of many sorts that are not always easy to distinguish. The results are obvious enough—we all know when we are in good places and when we are not—but it is far from clear when we have charted a course of action to help matters and when our energies make them worse.

There are places where one can come face to face with the monster we created with such vigor over the last fifty years and see what it is that we are now up against and how big it is. One such place is Interstate Highway 80, headed west from Auburn to Roseville, where the western slopes of the Sierra Nevada descend into the great Central Valley of California. To see the monster clearly, it should be a clear winter evening when it is dark during the time when traffic is at its peak. You are then part of an astounding human artifact that stretches downward and outward before you for twenty or thirty miles before it disappears into the mists. It is an unbroken ribbon of lights, pale orange on the left, bright red on the right, eight lights wide and twisty where the topography is still hilly, straightening and widening to sixteen lights wide where the valley goes flat. Tens of thousands of lights, half approaching, half receding, all moving at the same speed, equally spaced, without a gap. Henry Ford is purported to have said that there was no real demand for automobiles and that the market for them would have to be created. One can only imagine his response if he were confronted with this spectacle.

This slope between Auburn and Roseville is precisely the place where the cartographers of the 1830s and the settlers of the 1850s thought they had arrived in paradise, after they and their animals had made 5 million steps over the prairies and the mountains and through the seasons. It is where the builders of the Central Pacific, with Herculean effort, proved that the railroad could conquer the mountains and open California to settlement on a huge scale. Soon after the completion of the railroad, the vast grasslands that greeted the first settlers became an agrarian landscape more productive than any the world had known, and to many it was beautiful to behold from this spot.

Now it has changed again and is changing more rapidly all the time. All along the highway is the world as we have been constructing it for the last few decades. It would be hard to find anyone who thinks that anything about this latest episode of change is beautiful. The proverbial car dealer from the Libertarian Party might approve of this landscape, but even he would have trouble calling it beautiful. There are car lots—lots of them and big ones, brilliantly lit, and thousands of businesses that can be patronized only by car. There are franchise food places by the hundreds, malls and big boxes and residential planned developments, where people live behind sound walls on cul-de-sacs lined with garage doors. It is where well-being is measured by the number, size, and diversity of the vehicles one owns—the SUV, the Dualie, the snowmobile, the ski-boat, the dragster. It is not the kind of scene that is ever depicted in a travel poster for anywhere or an ad for anything. If advertising depicts aspiration, this seems not to be a place that even the people who built it aspire to inhabit.

If one knows a bit about tax policies, transportation plans (including those for rail), and the way that land use law and "planning" work in California, it is perfectly clear that, unless something changes, most of the vast Central Valley will look just like the I-80 corridor within twenty years and will contain a similar way of life. Every farmer and every municipality know the rules and know what they must do to survive. The incentives are for the farmers to cash out, and for each little hamlet to pay for its municipal services by building its own big box and automall. The bibliography explaining how and why this magnificent agrarian landscape is transforming itself into an endless ocean of edgeless low-density sprawl is long and compelling. The point here is not to repeat or paraphrase what all those books say but to cite their existence as proof that the fight against the monster is under way. It is a fight that is partially about public policy, tax law, and the techniques of planning but that is fundamentally about our deepest sense of how we want to live.

PART 2

TIMES

I will never forget the joy of the grown-ups when the Movie-Tone newsreel played the Air Corps anthem and the screen showed the cheering columns of Patton's 3rd Army in the snow on that famous Sunday in 1944, when the cloud cover lifted and the P-51s roared over their heads to break the siege of MacCauliff's gallant garrison at Bastogne.

To honor the Battle of the Bulge, my family made a Christmas tree. My parents were nonreligious Jews who thought there was nothing wrong with having a Christmas tree as long as it had nothing to do with Christianity. As a devout Freudian and a logical positivist, my father thought of religion as a form of mental illness that could be cured by modern science. Because it was wartime, there were no regular Christmas tree ornaments, so we decorated the tree with my private arsenal of war toys, which was perfectly in accord with my parents' sense of religious observance. Toy soldiers from the 101st Airborne hung on the tree from little parachutes made from cardboard egg cartons. Wooden tanks crashed through the snow of the Ardenne in the form of a sheet wrapped around the base of the tree. Above the paratroopers hung my collection of airplanes, including my favorite—my own silver and black P-51.

Until I was a fully grown, independent adult, all of my mentors and role models were people whose life experience had been shaped by the war. My high school football coach, Chad Reade, had flown a Grumman Hellcat off the USS *Hornet* and purportedly had shot down five Jap Zeros.

Every school day, promptly at 8:15, he would reenact his carrier landings by parking his battered 1951 Pontiac Silver Streak in one swift, deft backward maneuver that placed two sides of the car an inch or so away from an unprotected thirty-foot drop at the edge of the faculty parking lot. Each morning, a little group of admiring students assembled just to watch him park. I have never known anyone whose carriage and demeanor exuded heroism like Coach Reade's. I was a dedicated but small and deeply untalented athlete, and the principal thing I learned from him was unflinching physical courage, which over my high school and college years gave me a remarkably comprehensive knowledge of orthopedic injuries. Fortunately, one can outgrow courage of that kind. As with many things related to sport, one can find a vast metaphor embedded in this experience.

The spirit that dominated the building of the postwar world combined the qualities of Chad Reade with those of my father. Part of that spirit was a resolute and absolute fearlessness. Another part was belief in the rational, a complete faith in the ability of enlightened people to figure things out, just as they had figured out how to win the war. Part 2 contains reflections on those mentors and role models, people convinced of their own rectitude, rationalism, and heroism, who taught the young and built and rebuilt America in the decades after 1945.

Eichlers

In 1943, my father was an Army doctor at a base outside Sacramento, just west of where Interstate 80 now descends into the Central Valley. My parents made friends with three other Jewish families in town, whose breadwinners were respectively a furrier, a dentist, and an architect. The three families got together all the time to cook and eat, to play bridge, and to tell funny stories. The furrier lived in a bungalow with a porch and a great sloping front lawn. In the fall, we youngest children coated ourselves with sticky stuff—I think it was Johnson's Baby Oil—and rolled down the lawn to the sidewalk, ending up completely coated head to toe with sycamore leaves. The dentist, who had more money than the others, lived in paradise, a pink house on a corner in old Sacramento, with big screen porches, a swimming pool, and a rose arbor. The architect had a beautiful daughter named Missy, who was six months younger than I. I don't remember where they lived during the war, but shortly afterward, I think in 1949, they moved to one of the world's first mass-produced modernist suburban houses in an early Eichler subdivision outside Sacramento.

I will always remember the architect's pride as he conducted the first tour of his dream house for the other three families. In 1949, at age nine, I had my first encounter with the passions of an architect, and with the collective dream that architects shared about the postwar world they had just begun to build. For reasons I did not understand as a little kid, this speech about the canons of modernism—flowing space, the union

Inside utopia, Eichler interior

of mankind with nature, and the rationalization of production—entered the comedic lore of the other families, and all of the adults could do a version of it to the vast amusement of the others for years afterward. I began to see what was funny about five years later when Missy and I found the open plan of the architect's utopia an uncongenial setting in which to share the first gleams of hormonal dawn, and the indelible stolen moments of early adolescence took place instead in the furrier's cozy nooks and the dentist's magic rose arbor.

Joseph Eichler was the largest and most interesting builder of houses in Northern California after the war. By many ways of measuring, Eichler's houses are one of the great success stories of the postwar years, one of the few enduring cultural accomplishments from the days of Betty Furness and Arthur Godfrey. It is why they are cult objects today, like vintage racecars.

During the war years, there was very little work for architects. One exceptional individual, John Entenza, the sponsor and editor of *Arts and Architecture* magazine in Los Angeles, made work for many of the leading architects of the day imagining what postwar life might be like. Entenza and his distinguished stable of underemployed architects created the Case Study House Program, a fantasy during the war and a reality of limited scope afterward. The principal form giver for the Case Study aesthetic was Richard Neurtra, but other fine architects, such as Rafael Soriano and Pierre Koenig, also created beautiful modern houses of steel and glass with Entenza's sponsorship. The best known of the Case Study houses are glassy pavilions with flowing, continuous spaces and only the most delicate membrane separating indoors from out. Entenza's idea was to harness the artistry of the finest modern architecture and couple it with the most sophisticated industrial processes for postwar housing production.

The Case Study program was the precursor to Eichler, who studied its results, appropriated what he liked, and discarded what didn't work for him. Eichler also studied the works of William Levitt, whose Levittown was the model of rationalized mass production of housing for the G.I. Bill. Levitt had no interest whatsoever in the esoteric works of the best modernists but wanted houses, lots of them, that would be simple, pragmatic, and completely familiar to everyone. Eichler's own formula mixed equal parts of Entenza's Case Studies and Levittown, but the synthesis of the two was something quite different from either.

Postwar dreaming, Case Study House

Like Levitt, Eichler had no illusions about fundamentally changing the techniques or materials of home building. He saw correctly that the exquisite steel fabrication of the Case Study houses was a romanticized view of war technology that could never be adapted to housing on a large scale. But, like Entenza and unlike Levitt, Eichler believed that the aesthetics of modern architecture had a moral basis that masses of people could understand, respect, and learn to love. Eichler himself lived in a Frank Lloyd Wright Usonian house, and he saw himself as a missionary bringing the grace of modern architecture to a mass market. Eichler's houses look like modest versions of the Case Study houses, but they were made of timber, plywood, light wood framing, sheet rock, and particle board, not unlike the houses of Levittown.

The Eichler houses promised a lot, and they delivered a lot. Eichler promised a Frank Lloyd Wright Usonian house, a John Entenza Case Study house for Everyman, and he delivered it, more or less. He promised the union of house and landscape, he promised the light of the sun, and he promised the servantless house and the emancipation of the wife-servant—and he delivered all of them. Eichler promised tectonic truth, a house that was truly built like it looked it was built. He delivered the common house as an aesthetic morality play.

Curiously, the bungalows promoted in such journals as *American Craftsman* and *Bungalow Magazine* thirty years before promised exactly the same things and delivered none of them. The kitchens of Craftsman bungalows were dark and segregated; rooms didn't open to gardens, and the tectonic morality of the Arts and Crafts ideal was only there on the front porches, with their hearty posts, beams, and timber trusses exposed to view. The rest was light wood framing wrapped in cladding with a superficial symbolic language of trim masquerading as structure applied on top. Yet the bungalows also delivered something their purveyors were apparently totally indifferent to, or at least they never wrote a word about the subject in the decades in which their two journals were published. They delivered beautiful streets, common courtyards, neighborhoods, and communities—the American town at its noblest, most democratic, and most civil. Those quite, narrow, tree-lined streets—with robust front porches set back from them just a little, and the cars tucked behind, away from the street—are for many the archetype of American community. It is why bungalow neighborhoods are so popular today, and why people spend their money to remodel bungalows, opening up their plans and adding big sunlit kitchens on the back, so they have more of what Eichler's houses provided.

Eichler was an aesthetic missionary, and a successful one, but his noble accomplishment was part of something far from noble—the set of postwar policies that built our sprawling, isolating suburbs and wrought ruthless damage on our cities and city-regions. In addition to the qualities that Eichler's houses achieved so brilliantly, they also delivered something their creators never thought about, something destructive and more enduring than all they set out to do. Eichler's publicity photographs from the 1950s depict an entirely private world in which no two buildings reside next to each other, in which there is never a relationship to something older or different. Eichler's streets are the opposite of those in the bungalow neighborhoods. In his world, the porch-front street gave way to the carport, to dismal rows of them, which in reality most often have the totemic autos of the staged photographs displaced by the detritus of daily

The vanquished street, an Eichler garage

life. The private domain of the house is separated from the public one of the street by a filter of junk, and the only squeals of leaf-encased children one would ever hear are those encapsulated in one's own backyard.

The full scope of the comedy and the tragedy of the postwar suburban dream became the subject of lucid and devastating observation in 1958, with Jacques Tati's immortal film *Mon Oncle*. In this film, a classic French town, with all its quirkiness and street life, is torn down stone by stone to make way for something just like an Eichler subdivision. There is something amusing about many things that were hot stuff in the late 1940s and early 1950s, such as Raymond Loewy Studebakers, Chicken à la King, or women's hats with pheasant feathers. But what happened to cities and towns in those years is more tragic than amusing. Jacques Tati, with his hilarious but bitter lament over the fate of a town swept up in the building of the postwar world, may have been the first to be so prescient and so right.

Eichler was a man of his time, arguably a great man of his time, but the time and all that happened in the years right after the war were larger than he was. The grand things that Eichler accomplished did not survive Eichler the man. Without him as the force and the conscience, the art of the Eichler house quickly vanished. What did not vanish quickly, what was left for a later generation to struggle with, was the vanquishing of the street, the hegemony of the private over the public in an endless landscape of low-density, single-family sprawl, with streets lined with carports and nothing to walk to even if you wanted to. Frank Lloyd Wright and the Case Study architects imagined private utopias in which townscape would magically melt away. It was Eichler, and not they, who realized their dreams on a huge scale. He showed us that their dream, like so many other twentieth-century dreams come true, had its dark and nightmarish side. Eichler's legacy has left it to our generation and our successors to learn to build the American town all over again from scratch—like stroke patients learning painfully in their old age to walk and talk.

Three Eras

Most seven-year-olds have only a dim memory of being two and a half. For them, the period five years before lies across an unbridgeable gulf of history, lost in the mists of time. If one happens to have been born in late 1939, the experience of being seven was particularly odd, because it seemed that for everyone, grown-ups too, the period five years before lay across the same unbridgeable gulf of history. When people returned from whatever extraordinary way they had spent the years of World War II, the time before the war did not seem retrievable, nor did most Americans of the middle class have any desire to retrieve those struggling, doubt-ridden times. In many forms of endeavor there was no going back, but in no field was the sense of a decisive break, a total severing of the distant past of five years before, more complete than in town planning.

This abrupt severing of history had multiple causes, many of which are well documented. The stories of the G.I. Bill, the Federal Highway Act of 1949, and the actions of the Federal Housing Administration have been told by Kenneth Jackson in *Crabgrass Frontier* and later by James Howard Kunstler in *The Geography of Nowhere* and by Mike Davis in *City of Quartz*. They describe the public policies that kept the nation from sliding back into depression after the war but which also decanted the wealth of cities and built the postwar world of slum clearance, urban renewal, the suburban subdivision, the shopping center, and the highway.

But these public policies, vast and influential as they became, were only political and economic gasoline poured on a psychological fire. The war changed people. For so many, it was an absolutely unprecedented and life-forming experience of *competence*. My former teaching colleague Donn Reay was chief architect for the Royal Canadian Air Force in Greenland. By age twenty-six, he had built a city in a few months, a form of intoxication from which there is no recovery. My favorite movie as a little boy was *The Fighting Seebees*, starring Richard Widmark as the commander of a battalion of combat engineers, hacking down jungles and *building* their way across the Pacific.

The veterans returned from war in a stupor of hypercompetence, ready to build the world anew. And the places they returned to were the dingy cities of depression and neglect, where whole neighborhoods had not had even a coat of paint since the 1920s. The war economy had drawn millions of southern blacks to these neglected city neighborhoods, and the reaction of the veterans, the Richard Widmarks with their aviator shades and cigarettes dangling from their lips, was, "Tear it all down; build something else."

The new San Francisco, planned for better living, replaces the dilapidation and disorder of more than half a century. The rigid street system with its deathtrap intersections is reorganized, simplified. The indiscriminate mixture of commercial, industrial, and residential structures that is the disease of blighted areas is nowhere to be seen.

In this new city of space and living green there are no densely built-up blocks. Here no families live in murky cubicles, damp basements, rooms that are hardly more than closets. Public health nurses find no overcrowded households. No children or young people sleep in the same rooms with victims of tuberculosis. Nor do building inspectors discover unvented heaters, termite-riddled floors and walls. No conflagrations menace whole blocks of firetraps.

Gone are the disreputable joints, the so called smoke shops, hotels, and pool hall hangouts known to the police. Gone too are the alleys in which juvenile gangs plotted mischief that sometimes ended in murder. In the new neighborhoods of the Western Addi-

tion district the cost of municipal services is less than half of what it formerly was but San Francisco counts its gain in more than money—in greater civic pride, in better health, in lives saved.

The New City,
San Francisco Department of City Planning, 1948

In 1948, San Francisco planning director Mel Scott and his academic colleague T. J. Kent issued the document called *The New City*, which proposed tearing down *most* of the Victorian fabric of the city and replacing it with a big green space (at least a space represented by a big splotch of lurid green ink spread across two pages) with widely spaced slab buildings dotted around in it. The prologue to their report, quoted above, left no doubt as to what they thought of San Francisco. To them, the city of Dashiell Hammett and Sam Spade was not merely ugly—it was evil and degrading. One wonders where all the characters of *The Maltese Falcon* would have lived if the whole of their "New City" had been built. It is hard to imagine Sidney Greenstreet in a jogging suit enjoying that great swath of green ink that was to replace San Francisco. It took around fifteen years for a couple of dozen blocks of the Scott/Kent vision of a beneficent and moral place to be realized, but by then people were beginning to sober up from their postwar binge. They began to realize what is now generally known—that San Francisco was not so bad after all and that it was worth a coat of paint and some new electric meters and plumbing. The very parts of the city that Mel Scott and Jack Kent were so intent on tearing down more than fifty years ago are now among the most expensive large tracts of urban real estate in North America.

Jack Kent lived to be a very old man, well into his nineties, and I used to see him frequently, going in and out of the office he kept in the U.C. Berkeley College of Environmental Design. It seemed that he was neither a monster nor a fool, quite the contrary. He was a handsome, distinguished fellow in a baggy corduroy sort of way, always friendly, and I deeply regret never learning what he thought about things at the end of his life. Most of the big figures of the postwar years died off before they even had a chance to feel foolish, but Jack Kent went on and on for decades, doing good works for which he is remembered fondly. But at the end of his long life, what did he think about the ideas he pushed so vigorously in 1948? It would be so interesting to know, but I never figured out how to ask.

Jack Kent and his generation launched the second era of the American town. The whole evolution of American townscape can be divided into eras—a first era that begins with the earliest colonial settlements and ends at World War II, a second that extends from the war almost to the present, and now a new third era with the work of a current generation reacting to what was built on such a vast scale with such hubris, blind optimism, and disdain for history in the fifty years after the war.

The first era of the American town commenced when the great agrarian grids were drawn across the continent: the 640-acre sections and six-mile-square townships established by Congress in the East and the Midwest, and the Spanish land grants laid out according to the Laws of the Indies in California and the Southwest. Roads followed section lines, and section lines followed the compass through swamps and over hilltops, a transcontinental triumph of the abstract over the particular. Almost all of the builders of towns in the American West—the speculators, the hucksters, the railroad men, the missionaries, the visionaries—came with more or less the same idea of town fully formed in their heads. There were just a few who had different ideas, neo-baroque deviates like Pierre Charles l'Enfant and Augustus Woodward (planners of Washington and Detroit, respectively), and there was the romantic planning of Frederick Law Olmsted and his sons and followers, but for the most part, urban America shunned baroque diagonals and naturalistic wiggles. Our cities and towns of the first era were based simply and powerfully on an uninflected rationalist subdivision of the agrarian grid that served as an armature for real estate speculation and a grafting of the urban culture of Europe onto the wilderness. The grid of San Francisco is as ruthless to its topography as the agrarian grids of the hinterlands are to lakes and forests.

A number of milestones could serve as the birth date of the second era of the American town, but as good a date as any is the day in 1938 that the Federal Housing Administration (FHA) began work on a national planning code. The residential planning done by the FHA resulted in the FHA Minimum Property Standards (FHA-MPS), a document of incredible power that required obedience to its principles as a condition for federal mortgage insurance. This document shaped the whole explosion of postwar suburbia underwritten by the G.I. Bill.

The polemics behind the building patterns of the postwar world were born in the 1920s and evolved through many housing experiments of the 1930s. One of the main threads of thought from which these patterns derive was that of Clarence Stein and collaborators, Henry Wright and Charles Perry. Stein's fame is rooted in his Garden City projects of the 1920s: Sunnyside Gardens, New York, and Radburn, New Jersey. The impetus for these new towns was to decant the overcrowded, miserable slums of New York. For Stein, the very first principle behind these developments was "low-cost land, adequate in size, and easy of development." Among the influential disciples of Stein, Wright, and Perry was Rexford Guy Tugwell, part of Franklin Roosevelt's brain trust and first director of the New Deal's Suburban Resettlement Division. "My idea," Tugwell wrote in 1935, "is to just outside centers of population, pick up cheap land, build a whole community and entice people to go into it. Then go back into the cities and tear down whole slums and make parks of them." Here, with a spectacularly split infinitive, is the die postwar sprawl and decanting the life and wealth from American cities, as it was being shaped in Washington at the height of the New Deal.

The postwar template was based in part on the belief that American gridiron towns could not accommodate the automobile. The new codes of the second era imposed a pattern of enclaves in place of continuous urban fabric; traffic was restricted to arterials, and houses stood on curving cul-de-sacs. There is an interesting lineage to this pattern in the idealistic planning of Sunnyside Gardens and Radburn, which the great urban historian and New Yorker journalist Lewis Mumford had grandiloquently characterized as "a wider diffusion of the instruments and processes of high human culture, and ... the infusion into the city of the life-sustaining environment and life-directed interests of the countryside."

The planning of Radburn followed that of Sunnyside Gardens by only four years (1923 and 1927, respectively), but in those four years the culture of the automobile began to take hold decisively. At Sunnyside Gardens, parking is remote from houses in satellite garages. By 1927, this was an old-fashioned, unacceptable idea, and the Radburn Plan

41

alternates "footways" and "motorways," with the houses having two fronts, one with a small, private garage. The main front faced the footway, and another sort of front peeked past the garage at the motorway.

The footways are intended as the main public space of the town, leading to schools, athletic fields, and parks, which are commonly owned and maintained. Common or public ownership of the greenways was an essential part of the Garden City concept, and one of the prominent and vigorous champions of Garden City ideals during the New Deal, the writer and theorist Henry Churchill, made no secret that he believed in municipal ownership of *all* land. It was this emphasis on collective or public ownership of land that ultimately made the Garden Cities of the 1920s and 1930s unsustainable. As it turned out, stable and well-maintained communities could not be built upon the commitments of renters in the United States. The ideas of the Garden Cities movement, including public ownership of land and houses, were embraced by the federal government during the New Deal, and despite the formation of a large Greenbelt Town bureaucracy and the commitment of substantial federal funding, the Greenbelt towns did not become stable communities. It was mainly the people who planned them, not the residents, who had a sufficient stake in the Greenbelt Towns to give a damn about them.

If you attempt to rectify the problems of the Greenbelt towns by taking the plan of Radburn and make all of the land private except the streets, you destroy Radburn's principal social and physical ideas. You also cast the mold for the postwar subdivision, of which Joseph Eichler's are the most enlightened. Radburn houses had one-car garages and the two kinds of public realm: motorways and footways. Eichler houses, and all that followed, had two- or three-car garages or carports, with almost nothing peeking around them, and a real front that faced the private backyard. There is no public realm except the one for cars, no place for pedestrians and no destinations to walk to anyway. The postwar fate of the Garden Cities ideas that he had championed deeply depressed Mumford at the end of his life.

The second era of the American townscape took shape after World War II, as this privatized mutilation of the Garden City spread throughout the land. One of the important figures in housing immediately after the War was New Deal veteran Philip Klutznick, who had served Roosevelt and Truman as commissioner of the Federal Public Housing Authority. As part of the team that had built the Greenbelt towns, Klutznick knew their problems and set about rectifying them. He saw correctly that postwar housing needs created a massive opportunity for private investment, and in 1946 he formed American Community Builders (ACB) to plan and build the new town of Park Forest, Illinois, outside Chicago. The other members of ACB included Nate Manilow, Jerold Loebel, Normann Schlossmann, Israel Rafkind, Charles Waldmann, Joseph Goldmann, and Nathan Jacobs, all of them Jewish. These men, who had accomplished much through the New Deal and war years, chose not to put their energies into Chicago, where the established businessmen's clubs that had built the city for seventy-five years did not welcome Jews. The idea of new communities where those who had proved themselves so competent during wartime were not bound by the entrenched social structures of inner cities was one factor that gave impetus to suburbanization after the war.

What began in Park Forest, Illinois, and Levittown, New York, in 1946 reached its final form by 1965 with the advent of the business park, the introduction of the planned unit development, and the commercial triumph of the regional mall. By 1965, not only were the physical elements of the landscape of suburban sprawl fully formed, but an elaborate set of laws, procedures, financing mechanisms, underwriting criteria, and development practices to insure their perpetuation for generations was firmly in place. Street design standards, zoning laws, and the whole process by which development is financed made building according to the principles and procedures of the first era of the American town impossible and illegal.

Throughout America and now in many other parts of the world, one can see clearly the differences between the first-era town and the second-era town. California provides a particularly vivid example, because half of what exists in California today is relatively new—less than thirty-five years old. But half of it is not new. Much, in fact, is the record of California's great waves of settlement after 1850. Today the new parts and the old parts house the same culture and the same economy. People in Seal Beach, which is mostly old, differ little from people in Newport Beach, which is mostly new. San Franciscans may dress a little differently from people in Irvine, but they work at the same kinds of jobs and watch the same TV shows. Some nice old towns, such as the C&H Sugar town of Crockett, have died, but most old towns—big ones like San Francisco and little ones like Calistoga in the Napa Valley—have hung on and are doing just fine. Most people who live in the new places come to the old places all the time for things they don't have: streets where you can walk around, bars and cafés, music, theatre, and such. People who live in the old places tend to go to the new places only when they have to—for work or to go to the airport or places that discount tires.

Many people in the old places live in ways that were inconceivable at the time the old places were first laid out. They own cars. They shop in supermarkets. They work for large corporations that depend upon Broadband. They worry about security and getting from their car to their house without being mugged. They have sunlit kitchens, and sometimes they barbecue outdoors. Many of them like to exercise like mad all the time. The refitting of the first-era town so that modern life can take place within it is something that has occurred spontaneously throughout the world. California is one place that is half old and half new, half built before World War II and half after the war, and it is easy to compare this refitted second-era town with the first-era town. Many people go from one to the other every day and see the differences.

At this point, the deficiencies of the second-era town are no longer news. The congestion, isolation, tedium, and inequities of the postwar suburb have generated a whole bibliography of social criticism. Its ecological effects launched the environmental movement. Ugliness and the disaster of commuting—each has its own legions of critics. So many different aspects of postwar building patterns are viewed as serious problems by so many people in so many forms of endeavor that a third era of American town building is now under way. This new era was not launched on the tide of a great historic watershed like World War II or by a collective sense of having reached a single decisive moment from which there is no turning back. It grows from the cumulative experience and convictions of people in fields as disparate as water management and historic preservation, and from the scale of regional planning to that of urban infill on tiny lots. The foothold this new way of building has secured is a tenuous one, and its methods and conventions are still being formed. This new era of town making is based on appreciation and affection for many aspects of the first era of the American town, but it is not and cannot be just a re-creation of the time before World War II. Much too much has changed. Population pressures and the demographics of our cities are sharply different from years ago, the basis of our economy is different, and we must contend with and master the great transformative technologies that infiltrate every moment of our day and that our first-era ancestors never thought about.

The Dawn of Nonhistory

In 1948, spectators at the Big Game against Stanford in U.C. Berkeley's Memorial Stadium were amazed to see that, for the first time, the white-shirted Cal rooting section stretched from goal line to goal line. Pete Shabarum and Jim Monachino were the starting halfbacks. The immortal Jackie Jensen was at fullback, and speed merchant Paul Kekley was in reserve. What a time it was! The G.I. Bill was at its peak, and the campus was stuffed with temporary buildings. Opportunity was boundless; euphoria was in the air. The whole world was, as Winston Churchill had put it, "moving forward onto broad, sunlit uplands."

The first cognitive function that is impaired at times of intoxication is memory. In the glory times right after World War II, people forgot many things. The U.C. campus is a record of such a time—a huge physical reification of forgetfulness, a drunken stupor frozen in concrete. Enough of the prewar Berkeley campus remains to this day that it is easy to see that it was once a beautiful place, a strangely comfortable juxtaposition of Beaux Arts grandeur and Arts and Crafts folksiness, executed by people who clearly knew what they were about. Then, amidst all this, strategically at the very worst places, are the grossest, coarsest, most unremittingly banal concrete blockbusters from the 1950s. What were they thinking? Why are the ugliest, most dysfunctional and universally despised buildings on campus those that were built in the time of the greatest optimism, confidence, and prosperity the place has ever known?

The postwar builders on the Berkeley campus not only forgot that the campus had had a plan, quite a beautiful and sensible one, but they actually forgot what a plan was, how it was that people could go about the making and administering of a plan. One calls to mind places in Eastern Europe where suddenly, for some reason, late in the twentieth century people forgot how to make bread. To this day, remnants of the process, the structure, the methods of making decisions and allocating resources that emerged after World War II remain in force.

For the most part, the problem does not lie with the buildings themselves. The Haas Business School, the last building designed by Charles Moore, is a handsome piece of Arts and Crafts Revival, bisected by a monumental stair. The stair unfortunately ends not quite at a dismal back door to Wurster Hall, the College of Environmental Design. Wurster Hall's main courtyard, meanwhile, faces a parking lot. The university system has no budget category for the spaces that link buildings—only budgets for buildings. Each separate building constitutes a little fiscal and administrative cosmos unto itself—Bosnia, Croatia, Serbia, Montenegro, and so forth. Transportation, delivery, and parking initiatives proposed by the campus planning office are undone by departmental initiatives and interdepartmental squabbles. Everything is a piece at a time—programming, funding, designing, building, planting, serving, maintaining, replacing. The energies of planners, architects, facilities managers, deans, and users dissipate in a cacophony of cross-purposes and mutually negating agendas. There are dozens of faces—all grumpy— at every meeting about the smallest subject related to facilities or maintenance. The U.C. campus is, to put it gently, screwed up.

You don't have to go far from the Berkeley campus to find other big, complex, important institutions that systematically went about destroying themselves physically in the last half of the twentieth century. The Stanford campus is the same story, an even more glorious plan forgotten, ignored, and almost ruined in the binge of postwar construction. Stanford's original quads, with their mock Romanesque sandstone arcades, represent order and generosity in the making of public space that has been unthinkable in the last fifty years, a lost art. In the 1950s they built buildings at Stanford like Dinkelspiel Auditorium, which faces a parking lot with its broad, bare backside mooning the postwar era's pathetic and shapeless attempt at a public plaza.

Unlike the University of California system, however, Stanford entered the third era of American building—recovery from the mess of postwar craziness—more than fifteen years ago, and the results are heartening. Campus architect David Neuman (there actually *is* a campus architect) left the U.C. system, fully aware of its failings, and established at Stanford something called the Stanford Infrastructure Plan, or SIP. The SIP is a 9 percent assessment against the budget of every building that is specifically dedicated to the construction, repair, and maintenance of campus infrastructure and landscape. The existence of this fund, administered by the campus architect, makes the architect a real player, on equal footing with the facilities management bureaucracy and the people responsible for traffic, parking, and utilities. At Stanford, the awful wounds that the campus inflicted upon itself during its postwar psychosis have begun to heal, though not of course without considerable scar tissue. But Stanford is a much more handsome, coherent, and agreeable place than it was in 1980. Different architects, superstars included, have designed buildings that contribute to something larger than themselves, and there are spaces between buildings that make sense and are executed with care and intelligence. Stanford shows that recovery, even from the deepest illness, is possible.

The place in the Bay Area that shows the watershed of World War II most dramatically is not Stanford or the U.C. Campus but the San Francisco Presidio, the beautiful Army base that has been transformed into a national park. From the middle of the nineteenth century right up to World War II, the Army Corps of Engineers built things in the Presidio that have the highest status in the National Register of Historic Places—magnificent streets of porch-front brick houses, the splendid Mission Revival complex known as Fort Winfield Scott, stables, museums, all sorts of gorgeous stuff. Until 1940, it seems they could do nothing wrong; after 1945, they did nothing right. Scotch and martinis were popular in the years after the war and many people drank much more heavily than is common now, but what scotch and martinis do to people's livers is soothing compared to what postwar building did to the Presidio.

Now, as the Presidio is being restored, its buildings are classified in two categories: "historic" (before 1945) and "nonhistoric" (after 1945). The Presidio Trust and the National Park Service acknowledge that nothing built in the Presidio after 1945 is worth a damn and that virtually everything built there before 1945 is a national treasure. The housing built on the base in the late 1940s, 1950s, and 1960s is virtually identical to the public housing of the same era that was built all over the country and is now being torn down. Here, there will be an attempt to reuse much of it, because in a city where it is impossible to come anywhere close to satisfying the need for affordable housing, demolishing it seems like sinful waste. The real waste was building such egregious junk in the first place.

My contemporaries and I have an odd vantage point with respect to the postwar binge. We are old enough to have known many of the protagonists; most were about the age of our parents. But we are young enough to be immune to their enthusiasms, and many of us have spent our own professional lives reacting against what they did. But we did actually know many of the strangely interlinked cast of characters of the postwar reconstruction dramas, and we know that our own rebellion is gentle compared to the ruthlessness and contempt with which the postwar stars treated the prewar architectural establishment.

In 1948, shortly before William Wurster and his formidable wife, Catherine Bauer, set up shop as *the* power brokers in the interlinked worlds of architecture, planning, and design education on the West Coast, the renowned San Francisco architect Arthur Brown resigned the positions he had held for many years as the campus architect for both the U.C. Berkeley and Stanford campuses. Arthur Brown was the third campus architect at Berkeley, following George Kelham and the original planner of the campus, John Galen Howard. All three were products of the Ecole des Beaux Arts, and there was both a spirit and a set of formal principles that united their work across three decades. There was a clear direction under Kelham and Brown that the general sense of Howard's ideas needed to be honored, even as the campus went through changes that Howard never anticipated. Brown guided the campus through major growth in the twenties and thirties, and through the stylistic changes in the architecture of the Art Deco thirties, but he did not survive the tumult brought about by the return of the GIs.

To the postwar sensibility, Arthur Brown was *retardataire* beyond redemption. He was the architect of San Francisco's best and most important buildings—City Hall, the Opera House, Coit Tower, the magnificent

Temple Emanu El, the San Francisco Art Institute—but all of that accomplishment did not make a place for him in the years after the war; quite the contrary. Those great buildings were from *another time*, across the unbridgeable gulf of history. As the world entered what the Presidio Trust now calls the "nonhistoric" era, there is a fascinating crossing of paths in the plot lines of postwar biographies. When Arthur Brown left his two positions as campus architect, he and his southern socialite wife, Lurleen, headed off to Rome, where Arthur could get a dose of one of the things he missed so badly during the war years: the sublime works of his favorite architect, sixteenth-century mannerist Carlo Rinaldi. On their way to Rome, the Browns met an impressionable young Englishman named Colin Rowe. Fifty years later, Rowe would begin his memoir, *As I Was Saying*, with the tale of this encounter, which shaped his life. If people in America were as civilized as the Browns, it was a place he had to see. He went to Texas and then to Cornell, where he became the most eloquent voice calling for rethinking the ethos of modernist planning, under whose flag Arthur Brown was shown the door at Berkeley and Stanford.

The position of campus architect disappeared at both places when Arthur Brown left, replaced at Stanford by a hydra-headed bureaucracy and at Berkeley by a triumvirate of Wurster, university president Clark Kerr, and regent Ed Pauley. It was this trio that was in charge during the mauling of the previous generations of careful campus planning— soulless high-rises placed right in the principle view of corridors and public spaces, no two buildings having the slightest relationship to each other, and myriad other mindless blunders.

The teachings of Colin Rowe, meanwhile, helped to shape a next generation of American architects and planners whose proudest collective achievement to date is tearing down and replacing the public housing whose design standards and enabling legislation owed more to Catherine Bauer than to any other person. As Wurster's health began to fail around 1960, Berkeley found a place as distinguished visiting professor for Catherine Bauer's longtime old flame, Lewis Mumford. As I was beginning architectural studies at Stanford, I had the audacity to make an appointment with the great man during his required office hours. My impression was that of an unusually grumpy fellow, without much patience for an eager and naive undergraduate.

As is not well known, Mumford actually helped to design a physical plan during this period, the layout of buildings in Stanford's Escondido Village, with the first buildings done by Wurster's office. Escondido Village is a train-wreck type of plan, with one-story buildings scattered willy-nilly in a grove of trees. It is in every way the antithesis of the beautiful courtyards and monumental quads of the original Stanford plan. It wasn't so bad as a one-story encampment in the trees, but now, as Stanford students are pushed onto the campus in ever greater numbers by the Silicon Valley housing crunch, Wurster's shacky little units are being replaced by big permanent buildings, and Mumford's picturesque scattering is utter chaos. In 1998, our office won the invited competition to insert new dormitories into Escondido Village. What a strange little novel: Arthur Brown, William Wurster, Catherine Bauer, Lewis Mumford, Colin Rowe, and now us.

It is hard to find out what the people who wielded so much influence in the postwar years thought as they saw the havoc emerging around them. Mumford's late writings are tinged with bitterness, and Catherine Bauer accused him of self-pity. His attempt at Olmstedian planning at Stanford perhaps reflects a final position of anti-urbanism from the author of *The Culture of Cities*.

Bauer herself laid some of the groundwork for the movement that would begin to redress the public housing calamity that she had worked so passionately to help create. Some of her old public housing comrades felt betrayed by her at the end, but Jane Jacobs, the earliest, sharpest, and most effective critic of postwar town planning, had praise for Bauer's final positions: her advocacy of neighborhood planning as opposed to project planning and her recognition of the city-region as the fundamental physical and economic unit of the modern world. In the end, it was Bauer who was insightful and honest about what postwar euphoria had wrought. She wrote wistfully to Mumford:

> *You would have been an early Christian in the days of Roman decline, and I would not, and you would have been right . . . but I just can't blame people quite so much. I'm essentially a creature of the times, not a prophet crying in the wilderness, so I tend to have more sympathy than contempt for the rest of us, even our stupid leaders.*

Mumford was the champion of the Garden Cities movement, the twisted template of which became the pattern for the postwar sprawl that he detested. Bauer launched the public housing of the New Deal, which by the end of her life had become a trap for the poor and a deep scar all across the land. Mumford and Bauer lived through a time of vast change, and both had the rare intelligence to see how easily utopian dreams can produce dystopian realities so grim that they breed another generation of dreamers ready to tear down, rebuild, and try once more to get it right.

The Moderns

It is no mystery who the really cool people were in the years between World War I and World War II. They were people like Lewis Mumford, Catherine Bauer, Le Corbusier, Josephine Baker, Alfred Stieglitz, Georgia O'Keeffe, Duke Ellington, Albert Einstein, Picasso, Aaron Copeland, Gertrude Stein, Igor Stravinsky, Lester Young, James Joyce, and Charlie Chaplin. They were the people one would dream about being, or being among, if one could be transported to the 1930s in a time machine. Ralph Lauren has built his fortune on this fantasy, selling Mumford suits and Stieglitz khakis to aspirants to that brand of cool all around the world. These people were the modernists, proud harbingers of what was next, the remorseless enemies of staid convention. They carried such an air of conviction that the world they were capable of making was so much better, so very much more interesting than the world had ever been before.

The great achievement of the most influential architectural educators in the years just before and after World War II was their success in linking an architectural dogma to the heroism, irresistible cool, and sense of rectitude of these modernists. From the moment in 1937 that former Bauhaus director Walter Gropius became chairman of architecture at Harvard, his students had only to learn to draw or model widely spaced white boxes, carefully *not* learn anything about architectural history or how to make Beaux Arts watercolors, and they were already soul mates of the great ones, practically dinner guests of Stieglitz and O'Keeffe. That enduring mishmash of establishment careerism and avant-gardist posturing that Gropius learned to juggle so adroitly is his greatest legacy and is clearly as alive today as ever.

The success of the Bauhaus/Gropius/Harvard propaganda machine was truly astounding, but by no means accidental. Gropius eventually anointed his own revisionist court historian, Sigfried Giedion, who along with his colleague and contemporary Nicholas Pevsner, completely rewrote the hugely complex story of industrialization and urbanization in the nineteenth century. The gospels of St. Sigfried and St. Nicholas, the only architectural histories that most students of my generation were ever told to read, canonize a highly selected list of nineteenth-century engineers and architects as precursors in a divinely ordained revolutionary dialectic, leading to the building methods and stylistic preferences of (guess who) Gropius and his circle.

This cultural juggernaut, when added to the woes of the depression years, successfully brought to an end the careers of virtually the entire American architectural establishment of the 1920s. After World War II, people who had built great works in the 1920s, such as Ralph Adams Cram, Paul Cret, Bernard Maybeck, Arthur Brown, Irving Gill, and Julia Morgan, were still vigorous enough to have resumed working, but most of them never got the chance again. They were the old guard—discredited, irrelevant, irredeemably uncool. It is instructive and fascinating, however, to look at the few great cultural battles of the 1920s and the 1930s that were *lost* by the German modern architects and their progeny, who thought that the problems of the world could be solved by widely separated white boxes, the more austere the better. One of these battles was the vast housing program of the Marxist/Leninist Social Democratic Party in Vienna from 1919 to 1934.

There is so much we can and should learn from these buildings that we will return to them in more detail to discuss just why their formal organization and their spirit are so relevant today. The most famous of these great buildings, Karl Ehn's Karl Marx Hof, is now universally acknowledged as a canonical masterpiece, and I am the first to admit that its reflected luster shines on the best of my own works. What is interesting to note, however, is that it was considered a reactionary work at the time it was produced by those who became the avant-gardist establishment. The principal theorists and historians of the architectural academy, from

Sigfried Giedion in the 1930s to Manfredo Tafuri in the 1970s, dismissed it as a lost opportunity, a defeatist strategy in the struggle for modernity, definitely not cool.

The same can be said of other enduring works of the 1920s and 1930s that were outside the canons of modernism and had a finger or two in the classical past. Think about Deco skyscrapers in New York, or the best of Robert Moses's public works: the Central Park Zoo and the Brooklyn Heights Esplanade. Think about everything done by the Works Progress Administration, including that contender for the most magnificent of all human artifacts, Hoover Dam. And think about the great MGM musicals, decidedly outside the modernist canon, with more than two fingers linking MGM's famous choreographer and set designer, Busby Berkeley, to the aesthetics of the Beaux Arts. Despite the claims of the modernist court historians, there were very different cultural tracks running through those times, and one can't quite picture Walter Gropius as a dancing partner for Ginger Rogers. The cool people in the 1920s and 1930s did not do *all* the cool stuff.

Turning Twenty

Think what faced a twenty-year-old in 1960. Frank Mankiewicz, a high official in the incoming White House, announced that what Dwight David Eisenhower had done for golf, John Fitzgerald Kennedy would do for sex.

In New York at twenty, I could get standing room with my dancer friends and watch incredulously as Balanchine himself did Balanchine at the New York City Ballet, with Edward Villella as principal dancer. So hypnotic—those geometric, formal ballets—just bodies, just movement, just absolutely beautiful. This was the transcendent experience that religion is supposed to be about, but for my friends and me it wasn't any form of religion that did it. It was this blazing sense of modernity.

At home in San Francisco, as soon as I turned twenty-one, I could catch the late set at the Jazz Workshop and sit ten feet away from John Coltrane, the largest, darkest presence ever to fill a room. Coltrane just there, ten feet away, huge and black in his huge black suit, would take a solo and it would go on and on—thirty minutes, forty minutes, but forty minutes of eternity—an unbearable white light, like Hiroshima in your head, ten feet away, on and on and on. What could there possibly be after Coltrane? Like insects, we had to know what there could be on the other side of the light.

Architecture students at the beginning of the 1960s found their version of the white light in the late works of Le Corbusier, as crazy and spell-binding as Beethoven's last quartets. After such works, the world could never be the same. Like practically every architect in the world, I remember the overwhelming, life-shaping power of my own first real encounter with Le

Corbusier. In 1960, American students could bum around in Europe for less than it cost to stay at home. I had spent days looking for Le Corbusier's monastery of la Tourette. It was next to impossible to find, because the monks had cleverly kept the name La Tourette when they moved away from the village of La Tourette, precisely to escape people like me. To those who succeeded in overcoming their ruse, they were friendly enough, and I was allowed to wander all through that incredible place. I remember standing transfixed outside the bright green metal door of a raw concrete monk's cell, listening to Stravinsky booming away on the other side of the door. The strength, the austerity, the sheer genius of every space and every vista were enough to give a twenty-year-old the dilemma of whether to become a monk or to become an architect. The downside of monkishness was clear enough, that of architecture less clear, so my fate was sealed.

For all of us, who as kids had moments like that outside the green door, there could be no backward glances, no sentiment, no failure of the valor it took to proceed into the unknown. So we followed that magnificent crowd of the coolest people ever, the final moderns: Coltrane, Balanchine, Le Corbusier, Jackson Pollack, whose careful explosions of paint were like the works of those physicists who had unlocked the energy of the stars.

We followed the last moderns because we had to be the ones after them, the ones to discover the world on the other side of the light. What we could not know was that we had arrived at the festival in the final hysterical blaze of the fireworks. Soon, very soon, it would be over, and there would be a long, slow, painfully slow dawn, and we would see, dimly at first, and bit by bit more clearly, what was left, what had been wrecked, what had been neglected in the Dionysian frenzy of our elders, and we would see the overwhelming work that lay ahead—our lifework.

When it was finally light, we saw the world after Balanchine, after John Coltrane, after Jackson Pollack, after Le Corbusier, after the final moderns, after Jack Kennedy, after Bobby Kennedy and Martin Luther King, after the craziness between the pill and AIDS, after Viet Nam and 1968, after dope got really ugly and after they blew up the public housing at Pruitt-Igo, because it was one of the postwar dreams turned nightmare that dynamite could get rid of.

Deliverance at the White Table

The only real live, walking, breathing German Modernist from the 1920s I ever met was Konrad Wachsman. A visit to his Building Science Laboratory at the University of Southern California around 1970 was like going to Jurassic Park. Wachsman was the dinosaur, thundering around the place, an awesome, formidable creature from another time, implausible but very much alive. He was an architect, but his "laboratory" was the essence of the kind of architecture Denise Scott Brown had in mind when she coined her memorable phrase "physics envy." The students who worked there were Ph.D. candidates in his special program, and the place was stuffed with projects that looked like props for *Dr. Evil Conquers Mars*.

The project that Wachsman was most proud of was something called "the translational rotational deflector." It was the work of a six- or seven- person team that included a structural engineer, a metallurgist, and a physicist in addition to several architects. Their task was to build a large, mechanized version of a little paper construction that Wachsman had made himself. The paper object was a white cube, ten inches on a side with a little mechanism inside. The property of the mechanism was that it could locate any two points within the cube. It could stretch, shrink, and always maneuver out of its own way so that the two points could be anywhere inside the cube. Wachsman seemed to have lots of money from industry or NASA or somewhere to subsidize the project. The students' version was ten feet on a side and operated to an accuracy of .001 inch. Apparently, the hard part was getting it to be so accurate, and it involved mechanical, thermal, and production problems that took the team years to figure out. The white walls were absolutely flawless, and the mechanism inside was made of exquisitely machined alloys of stainless steel. Outside the cube was a stainless steel control panel with row upon row of switches, dials, and lights. It made a big humming noise when it operated. It was very, very impressive, as were most of the other projects in the huge loft space next to the L.A. Coliseum, across the road from the School of Architecture.

Wachsman detested the question of whether there was an *application* for an instrument like the translational rotational deflector. His response, delivered in a voice intended to make the questioner melt through the floor, was, "Before there was Mozart, there was the harpsichord." That may or may not have made much sense, but the effect was withering nonetheless.

Very shortly before Wachsman died in 1978, he came to Berkeley to give an evening lecture he called "1001–2001." A few of the faculty regarded him as an important figure, kind of a missing link to the original and heroic aspirations of the modern movement, and the lecture hall was packed with students dutifully honoring their teachers' requests that they attend. The lecture began at 8:00, and by around 10:30 he had gotten from the year 1001 to 1400. Four hundred years in two and a half hours, with six hundred big years left to go! The students left in droves. A few of us remained, scattered around the empty room to listen for hours more to this strange, inchoate, fascinating ramble—part bitterness, part gossip, part ideas of incredible range and audacity, part just totally nuts.

He told in excruciating detail the story of his nine-year exodus from Germany to the United States. He had been at the Bauhaus in its greatest days, apparently not exactly as a faculty member nor really a student but, by his own account, on intimate terms with the most famous figures: Walter Gropius, Mies van der Rohe, Lazlo Moholy-Nagy, Johannes Itten, Hannes Meyer. In 1937, when all the others finally left, some for the Soviet Union, most to fancy teaching jobs in the United States, he too fled but got only as far as Paris. There he could find nothing to do that was remotely related to his architectural dreams and for nine years supported himself doing this and that, mostly working as a waiter.

Finally, in 1946, Walter Gropius, in his capacity as chair of architecture at Harvard, arranged a visa and invited him to Cambridge. Wachsman recounted each step of the journey, to New York by ship, then directly by train to Boston, then by cab to Gropius's famous house in Lincoln, Massachusetts, arriving at one in the morning. Ise Gropius had cabled him instructions how to find the house and how to let himself in the back door, if he arrived late. He entered the back of the house into a breakfast room and found a light switch that turned on a glass fixture that he recognized as the work of one of the Bauhaus stars. The lighting fixture hung over a round, white laminated plastic table that he remembered being made in the Bauhaus shops by Lazlo Moholy-Nagy. He was overcome with emotion, even at the retelling of this story thirty-five years later. Like someone recounting a drug experience, he described the feeling of the warmth and the wetness of the tears between his cheek and the white plastic tabletop.

Decades after a round, white laminated plastic table became as commonplace as a drink of water, it could stand as symbol for all that is deficient in the man-made world that accompanied it, the very paradigm of absolute, universal featurelessness. But think what a drink of water is to someone dying of thirst. That was the condition half a century ago to those for whom it was a different kind of symbol, standing for nothing less than a culmination of the enlightenment, a messianic age of collective redemption through the union of science, art, and industry. That is what they thought about, those old dinosaurs, and when one understands that, one can begin to make sense of their hubris, their ruthlessness, and their tears.

Panic

My first year as a twenty-seven-year-old assistant professor at Berkeley was filled with frenzy and moments of heart-stopping anxiety. In that year, I also undertook my first independent architectural commissions. A young architect's first house is like most people's first sexual experience—the culmination of an apparently endless period of fantasy, preparation, and anticipation. One's entire persona is wrapped up in the outcome, *so it better be good*. I worked with a slightly older friend named Colin Wright, who I *thought* had more than my meager knowledge of how to put buildings together. Together we devised a neat system of hillside construction, made of big timber posts and beams. We thought it was absolutely radiant with Tectonic Truth, which we, as products of good architectural schools, thought was a virtue of the highest order. We believed to the bottom of our souls in the morality of its intrinsic thinghood.

One day, when the house was partially built, the contractor called and said that I needed to meet with the electrician. Colin was not around. The electrician was a crusty old bird, and he walked around the half-built house with a strange appraising look. "Very interesting," he said, "the way you have exposed all these posts and beams and structural decking—but where do you run wiring in this kind of a house?" My mouth fell open, and every organ between my esophagus and my bowels went into spasm, I managed to ask weakly, "You mean . . . *you* don't know?"

The second wave of panic came when the academic year started (fall 1967) and I learned that I would be teaching a lecture course for two

hundred students that met three times a week. At that point, the sum total of my knowledge and thoughts about every subject in the world could
have been stated nicely in about an hour and a quarter, so what was I going to do with *thirty hours* of lectures to two hundred people?

The most anxious moment came at the end of the academic year
in June, when I was summoned to the office of Dean William Wheaton.
Wheaton was a very distinguished, impressive man with whom I had ex-
changed two words and one handshake back in September. In his office,
he was seated behind a big imposing desk, and I was offered the kind of
spindly chair that leaves you with the question of what to do with your
hands. He began the conversation by telling me that he had leukemia and
that morning had had all of his blood changed. He knew he couldn't last
much longer, but he felt fine after his transfusions.

While I was processing this information and trying to figure out
the least graceless way to respond to it, he picked up what appeared to be
my personnel file. " It says here," he said peering over an elegant pair of
half glasses, "that you are the chairman of the Wurster Hall Public Spaces
Committee. I know you have been busy, but it appears that this committee has not had a single meeting all year."

I think my poised and articulate retort was something like "ulp"
or "glub."

"I'm going to give you a chance to make amends," he said. "Can you
design the base for a piece of sculpture?"

"Oh, yes," I said. "I can do that just fine."

He took a big tape measure out of a drawer and pushed it across the
desk to me. "First," he said, "you have to measure Catherine." He then
unveiled a bust of a lively looking middle-aged lady, which the inscription
identified as Catherine Bauer Wurster. I learned later that this was the second casting of the bust by Oscar Stonorov that stands in the lobby of HUD
in Washington. After I had measured her every which way and dutifully
recorded the measurements, he said, "Now, you have to measure me.
Catherine is going to live in the Environmental Design Library. I have the
key to the library. Every night I want to kiss her good night, on the forehead, so measure me and get the base just the right height." He stood and
leaned forward, and I measured the exact distance from the floor to his

lips. My high anxiety suddenly melted into this touching moment of incredible sweetness.

My god, what was there about this woman that would make this august man go to such pains to be able to kiss her effigy on the forehead each night of his last months on earth?

I had first learned about Catherine Bauer Wurster at the time of her death, two years before. I was working for the landscape architect Lawrence Halprin on a joint venture they were doing with Wurster, Bernardi, and Emmons. We were working in a miserable basement connected to the rest of the world and the Wurster office upstairs by a loudspeaker system. The other young denizens of this lowest level of architectural purgatory included Arthur Gensler, founder and now CEO of one of the world's largest architectural firms; Sandy Hirshen, later dean of architecture at the University of British Columbia; and Christopher Alexander, author of *The Pattern Language, The Timeless Way of Building,* and *The Nature of Order.* On a Monday morning, the loudspeaker informed us that Mrs. Wurster had not returned from a Sunday afternoon hike and that people from the office would be out because they were part of a search party. In an increasingly despairing voice, the loudspeaker kept us informed throughout the day about the search for this woman, whom we youngsters knew of only as the wife of the man desperately ill with Parkinson's disease that we saw being wheeled into the office each day.

I don't remember whether it was late that afternoon or Tuesday morning that the loudspeaker informed us, "The search is over." Catherine Bauer Wurster's body had been found on a remote spot on Mt. Tamalpais above Stinson Beach. I do remember a wailing explosion of grief, like the funeral of a martyr, broadcast to us through the loudspeaker. Later, as we mingled on the street with the people from upstairs, it was clear that this terrible grief was genuine on the part of the senior people who really knew Mrs. Wurster, and perhaps a little feigned by people who knew her less well. Without doubt, there was something special about this woman.

I heard fragments of her remarkable story over many years, but it was not until the publication of Peter Oberlander's biography, *Houser,* in 2000 that I learned how the fragments fit together and how extraordinary she really was. In 1932, when she was just twenty-six years old, she was hard at work on writings that became *Modern Housing,* the classic book that laid the groundwork for the New Deal's program of public housing. She published articles in *Fortune,* the *Nation, New Republic,* and *Arts Weekly.* She also curated the much-praised housing section of the Museum of Modern Art's seminal *Modern Architecture: International Exhibition.* In the midst of all this, she found time to conduct her long and torrid affair with Lewis Mumford, who was at the peak of his career and very much a married man. This routine must be a still-standing world record for precocious brilliance and perhaps for sheer energy. *Houser* contains excerpts from the correspondence she carried on with Mumford until the end of her life, and it is fascinating to read Mumford's somewhat ponderous attempts to animate the normal gravitas of his prose to keep up with the ruthless psychological acumen and unbridled sexual gaiety of her amazing letters.

It was her brilliance and energy that so captivated Bill Wheaton's dying heart and that had propelled the things she believed in into the mainstream of American public policy. Her passions and her legacy were shaped by two long European trips she made between 1929 and 1932. On these trips, she met many of the brightest lights among the architectural avant-garde of Germany, Holland, and France, saw their work, and became completely swept up in what they were trying to do. Their message became her mission for America.

Catherine Bauer's European journeys and Le Corbusier's 1935 trip to America were essential elements of the cross-fertilization of European ideas and American opportunity that produced the dominant conventions of city building in both the United States and Western Europe after World War II. As one reads accounts of these seminal voyages of discovery, one cannot fail to notice some striking similarities. For one thing, both of these remarkable people were, by today's standards, wildly promiscuous. Almost everywhere they went, both of them seemed to have someone new and interesting to jump in the sack with. In the 1930s, it seems, being modern was lots of fun. Sexual liberation was a great emblem, worn like a merit badge, standing for a larger liberation from the proprieties, stuffiness, and artistic canons of the *ancien régimes.*

It is tempting to speculate what the history of American public housing and urban renewal might have been had Catherine Bauer's journeys taken her to Vienna instead of Amsterdam, Berlin, and Frankfurt. What if it were Viennese, not German and Dutch, housing models that were introduced by her through the Museum of Modern Art in 1932? What if reconstruction and modification of the traditional city as it was practiced in Vienna, not eradication and replacement as the German, Dutch, and French modernists preached, had been introduced to America with the same vigor and brilliance? What if the housing legislation of 1937 written by Catherine Bauer had championed Viennese, not German, models. Perhaps there would be no need fifty years later to tear down all that was built. Perhaps, as in Vienna, the public housing of America would have been a cherished, impeccably maintained address for generations of working poor, new immigrants, disabled citizens, and others.

I have never known anyone who wielded the power over others that Catherine Bauer Wurster did. She was much too smart not to have known that her great quest and that of her proud, heroic generation ended so very badly. Surely there is some inextricable connection between the high moral purpose of my first posts and beams and the infectious vigor of Catherine Bauer Wurster's convictions. They are two sides of that flawed but totally compelling modernity that we have yet to fully understand or recover from.

Erasure

An entire generation believed that it was possible to build something that was fundamentally better than the American city. Not just architects and planners, but ordinary citizens, were convinced that the city they inherited was a reliquary of buildings and ideas from some distant and deeply irrelevant prewar past. Public housing, urban renewal, and most of the urban planning codes written between the late 1940s and the 1970s were swept up in this belief.

It is possible to look at the difference between the postwar American city and traditional town building as it was practiced in America until World War II in a very simple, reductive way. In traditional town building, there is a sharp distinction between monuments or public buildings and the ordinary fabric of the town. Monuments are special, and town fabric is normative—not special.

Town fabric in a traditional town has three distinctly different roles that must be reconciled with one another. First, it houses people and provides places for their work and for their private needs—security, daylight, privacy, whatever. Second, town fabric creates the settings for monuments. Without a setting of town fabric, monuments like churches or town halls lose their symbolism and their meaning. Third, town fabric shapes and defines the outdoor public spaces of a town—the streets, squares, and courtyards where town life traditionally takes place. Reconciling these three roles of town fabric has never been a simple matter, and in many American cities under the pressures of immigration and industrialization, it was the first role of town fabric—accommodating the private needs of people—that was compromised to the point of disaster. The first generation of American housing legislation, the New York Tenement Laws of 1901, dealt with the most egregious problems of town fabric as habitation and the health and social problems that were bred in tenement housing, without adequate light and air.

The modernist planning imported to the United States from Europe in the 1930s was a response to similar conditions of overcrowding and disease in industrial slums. These ideas, which formed the basis for the second era of the American town after the World War II, saw the complex compromise demanded of town fabric in traditional town building as an inherently flawed proposition. By eliminating the distinction between fabric and monuments and subjecting all buildings to the same rational planning and problem solving, modernist planners and architects believed that the social ills of the industrial slum could be designed away. They also believed that nothing short of a complete eradication of the hopeless and fundamentally wrong-headed patterns of American cities would do the job.

It was this hubris and optimism that led public housing and many other kinds of public and private initiatives to embrace an architecture of erasure. What the architecture of erasure erased was, in fact, the history of American urbanism, the record of the way American cities were built from their first settlement until World War II. Everybody knows the rest of the story, what a hated specter of dread this architecture of erasure became, what political forces it unleashed in cities. In my town, what was erased wherever people managed to do it was the original platting that gave San Francisco its structure and character—these powerful imaginary lines drawn on the ground by the surveys of 1837, 1847, and 1849, the city grid, its pattern of lots and the architectural character that evolved directly from them. What it also erased was the history of tiny interventions, the subscale of courts and alleys that make San Francisco a city that people love.

The architecture of erasure seemed so rational, so based on putting structural and mechanical components together in sensible ways, on optimal patterns of daylight, on building lots of units cheaply and quickly with a minimum of drawing, and fussing—so like the way we had won the war. It seemed so beneficent and liberal for the government to provide in a systematic, rational way what the marketplace had done haphazardly and irrationally, or not at all in the case of the poorest citizens. That is what the best of the German *Zeilenbauen* that Catherine Bauer so admired had accomplished, and they were her dream for America.

By 1975, however, the deficiencies of the architecture of erasure were no secret, and the great failures of the postwar experiments were commonly acknowledged. "Urban renewal" was a dirty word, many public housing projects had turned into hell holes, freeway fighters had stopped the highway builders in some cities, the historic preservation movement was in full swing, and in many places neighborhood groups had newfound muscle over the development process.

In 1975, my teaching colleague Anne Vernez Moudon began writing a book on how San Francisco was built, called *Built for Change.* The spirit of this book reversed the attitudes that had motivated most academic planning studies for the previous fifty years. This was not a quest for a better world. It was a reverent and analytical study of the residential fabric of a city that clearly had enduring worth.

The reasons people (and the real estate market) place such value on San Francisco's historic fabric are clear enough. However messed up San Francisco may be, physically and politically, it is still a beautiful place and its structure and scale nurture important things that people need from cities. It is a pattern of settlement that both orients people in the world and connects them with one another. The odd combination of steep hills, view corridors along straight gridiron streets, and water on three sides makes San Francisco one of those cities in which you have a clear sense of a large and distinctive terrain and of where you are within it. The particular geographies of Rome, Stockholm, Hong Kong, Vancouver, and Rio de Janeiro locate you in similar ways. And as in any good city, many of San Francisco's streets are well-defined public places, congenial for walking.

Its physical structure and its impact on people's consciousness are the inverse of the second-era town that emerged after World War II, with its big roads and segregated zoning of residential enclaves, public housing, shopping centers, and business parks. Unlike the wiggly roads and massive grading projects of the suburbs, San Francisco's regular, almost uninflected grid was laid over the hilly topography in a way that did not obliterate it. In San Francisco, one has a sense of being located not only in space but also in time and connected to the story of the building of the place. The city doesn't have a long history, as do Rome and Jerusalem, but like those cities, the record of its past is right before your eyes and part of everyday experience. And like all of the great and memorable cities of the world, San Francisco doesn't look like anyplace else. *Built for Change* records a pattern of building that grew out of a unique circumstance that has never been repeated elsewhere.

San Francisco has neighborhoods, places with names and boundaries. Its streets are defined by consistent building types of a scale that is big enough and dense enough to feel like a real city but small enough to be comfortable and intimate. And it has a whole network of small places to discover—alleys, courtyards, staircases like in Rome and Hong Kong, where the public way is too steep for streets. It has neighborhood parks embedded in the city fabric and surrounded by housing like London's, providing places for children, nannies, old folks, anyone. Most important is the possibility or likelihood of encountering almost anyone; that is what cities provide.

Observation of these qualities hardly registers as a great epiphany today, and it seems incredible that an entire generation, including its best and brightest, forgot about them altogether. Politicians, planners, architects, developers, bureaucrats—everybody—just forgot. Societies have their weird periods in which almost everyone plunges lockstep into something that seems like collective madness the moment it is over. Then nobody can quite explain how it happened. Germany had its Third Reich; China, its Cultural Revolution. We had the architecture of erasure—not quite so crazy, but crazy enough.

As Anne Vernez Moudon was working on her pathbreaking book, I found myself dealing with the same subject. By then, everyone agreed that the San Francisco Planning Code was a big mess. It had been written for the most part in 1961, and like most planning codes in American cities, it incorporated what were considered the essential truths of modern city planning: sunlight was good, large lots were better than small ones, different uses should be separated from one another, streetscapes didn't matter, and density and lot coverage were the ways you measured the qualities of buildings. This code was simultaneously vague and prescriptive. On one hand, it didn't seem to say much; on the other, it was definitely producing a new kind of city fabric, one that nobody seemed to like because it bore not the slightest resemblance to the city it was intended to be part of. And, though nobody in 1975 defended the 1961 Planning Code, no one had come forward with an idea about how to change it. Through an odd confluence of naiveté and the freedoms that go with a teaching job, I found myself in 1975 with a small National Endowment for the Arts grant to help the San Francisco Department of City Planning rewrite the rules. The work we (principally Mark Winogrond of the planning department and I) produced was a proposal for some twenty-eight changes to the Planning Code based on simple, commonsense observations about the differences between the old city fabric that people liked and the new one that people detested. Its prescriptions included things like limiting the amount of building front that could be devoted to garages and driveways, requiring that buildings step down the hills at the frequency of the original lot lines, and requirements about the frequency of building entrances along streets. This work had the catchy title "Change Without Loss" and was done without any precedents we knew about or a supporting theory other than some passages in Jane Jacobs's *The Death and Life of Great American Cities* and the illustrations and early drafts of *Built for Change*.

"Change Without Loss" may not have been a watershed in the history of the city, but it did represent a personal enlightenment of sorts for me, and it set a direction. It was followed by a demonstration project, Pacific Heights Townhouses, that I designed for a group of clients intent on showing that new housing in San Francisco neighborhoods did not have to wreck the place and that developers could actually make money by building in a way that would be liked by the preservationists intent on saving the city.

PART 3

SITE VERSUS ZEIT

A central feature of modernity is an obsessive preoccupation about time. Modernism revolves around a belief that cultural expressions of all sorts—and architecture and the design of objects particularly—owe allegiance to an elusive essence of the time of their production, an essence that is distinct from that of all previous times. If a work of art or an object anticipates the essence of a future time that is just over the horizon, that is to the good, because another essential feature of modernism is the idea of progress. New models are bound by the dialectics of history to be better, or at least more appropriate to the times, than the old ones. This attitude was born during the period of explosive industrialization and urbanization in the mid- to late nineteenth century. Never before had technological change been so rapid, and never before had the texture of people's lives been so affected by new technologies. Under these conditions, it seemed absurd to clothe the artifacts of the new industrial society in the trappings of cultures that were eight hundred or two thousand years old. Corinthian telephones and Gothic railroad bridges seemed profoundly silly.

By the last quarter of the nineteenth century, it had become the central mission of architecture, town planning, and the decorative arts to seek out new forms for the new times; for many, that mission has not changed to this day. In 1960, as my own interest in architecture and modernity took form, I read and reread Sigfried Giedion's *Space, Time and Architecture,* a book sponsored by Gropius at Harvard in 1941 as the modern movement's official party line regarding its own history and evolution. Giedion's principal idea was that human perception had been profoundly and permanently altered by two cataclysmic and intertwined ideas at the beginning of the twentieth century: Einstein's theory of relativity and synthetic cubism as practiced by Picasso and Bracque. To Giedion, these ideas were the culmination of lines of thought that had evolved for centuries and were destined to shape all aspects of culture as profoundly as discovery of the laws of perspective had shaped the humanism of the Renaissance. To my generation of students, these were intoxicating notions.

Also in 1960, the California Division of Highways built the Embarcadero Freeway along the San Francisco waterfront. I loved the freeway, because I thought that zooming a couple of feet away from buildings at seventy miles an hour was a validation of what Giedion was talking about:

> In order to grasp the true nature of space the observer must project himself through it. . . . Space in modern physics is conceived of as relative to a moving point of reference, not as the absolute and static entity of the baroque system of Newton.

When people said that they hated what the freeway did to the city, how it ruined the waterfront, how dark, dirty, and noisy it was, I thought they just didn't get it. They had not even *read* Giedion. They had failed to become kinetic observers, and they were stuck in modes of perception that were completely out of date. I believed that not liking the Embarcadero Freeway in 1960 was like not liking Picasso in 1914, a short-lived philistine rejection of a prophetic but not yet familiar way of seeing.

Things are different now. The Embarcadero Freeway is gone, wrecked by the Loma Prieta earthquake of 1989 and replaced by a beautiful palm-lined boulevard. The freeway had a few supporters who liked its convenience, but almost everyone rejoices in its absence, and certainly no one worries about kinetic observers or modern modes of perception. It is not possible to find a single San Franciscan who valued the Embarcadero Freeway because it embodied the identity of the times.

The identity of the times was a nineteenth-century cultural problem that is no longer a burning issue. In a society cast adrift on a sea of ever-changing news, the menus, the clothes, the music, the software of ten years ago are totally dated. A Golden Oldie is twenty years old, and people do not confuse the 1970s with the 1980s. In information culture, time—even small increments of time—is instantly recognizable. The immediate worldwide dissemination of information, products, and style creates an opposite sort of problem—not the identity of the time, which is inescapable, but the identity of place. What our world threatens more fiercely than it threatens the ozone layer or biodiversity is the concept of place, something our millennial ancestors always depended upon and took for granted. It is the blurring of difference between Jakarta and Glendale that is our generation's special problem.

For a long time, some people who engaged in architecture and town planning have recognized this fundamental shift in the challenges facing their disciplines. At the tenth meeting of the Congres Internationaux d'Architecture Moderne (CIAM) in 1950, a splinter group, calling themselves Team X, formed to challenge fundamental precepts of the architectural and town planning theories that were shaping postwar Europe. One of the leaders of Team X was the Dutch architect Aldo van Eyck, who formulated a specific challenge to Giedion's grand abstraction, stating that the fundamental task of postwar construction had to do with "place and occasion," not "space and time." Following the lead of the Team X architects, the Norwegian architectural historian and theorist Christian

Norberg-Schulz developed an argument about the importance of place, based in large part upon Martin Heidegger's most explicit consideration of architecture, his 1951 essay "Building Dwelling Thinking." Norberg-Schulz's *Genius Loci: Towards a Phenomenology of Architecture* is a poetic evocation of the particular magic of places and remains a pivotal book. In the United States, MIT planning professor Kevin Lynch initiated a Heideggerian line of inquiry, embodied in his influential *Image of the City,* published in 1960.

Despite the cogence of their arguments, however, these *place-niks* have been a relatively marginal force in the architectural academy and architectural practice until recently. Modernism, with its Zeitgeist dreams of a universally applied rationalism devoted to the essence of the times, captured the academy at the end of the 1930s and dug a set of defenses so elaborate that it will not be dislodged just by the anachronism of its main premise. Norberg-Schulz and Lynch have had their devotees at schools that much of the design establishment considers stodgy, such as Berkeley and MIT. The most powerful levers of influence, however, those that connect Harvard, Columbia, Cooper Union, and London's Architectural Association with the museum world and the architectural press, have remained squarely in the hands of the Zeitgeisters, from the late 1930s to this day. At all of these institutions, time still obliterates place.

An interesting and important exception to this rule has been Yale. There, the deanships of Charles Moore (1965 to 1970), Fred Koetter (1993 to 1998), Robert A. M. Stern (1998 to the present), and other teachers and administrators, such as Alan Plattus, have connected this influential school to architecture's role in re-creating the unique identities of particular places and have identified that role as a cultural mission of the deepest significance.

There has been enough theorizing about the importance of this cultural mission in the new global information age to give it a coherent operational program. However, this body of theory has not been sufficient to dislodge what are essentially nineteenth-century ideas about modernity from their central and controlling place in the architectural world. It is a long struggle that was begun by Van Eyck and Norberg-Schulz many years ago. The job is not complete, because the Zeitgeisters are a stubborn lot, like the cockroaches in a New York kitchen. No matter how much Colin Rowe you spray on their Hegelian dialectics, they just keep on coming.

The essays that follow in Part 3 are part of the job Aldo Van Eyck began and many others have continued, to help the ever more relevant idea of place to stand on at least equal footing with the now much less urgent idea of time.

Colin Rowe

Many people encounter something in their lives that they can never get out of their heads. It lurks like a shadow behind everything they do or think after the encounter. My personal encounter was my first reading of *Collage City* by Colin Rowe and Fred Koetter in 1977.

At that point, I had been practicing architecture on my own and teaching for ten years. After trying a lot of this and that, I was finally getting my feet on the ground and finding what seemed to me a direction that made some sense. It all had to do with San Francisco and the fact that virtually everything that had been built since World War II in the city I had grown up in, lived in, and had great affection for seemed harmful to the city and made it a less good place. This included a lot of building: all of the federally funded urban renewal of the 1960s, all of the City's public housing, the freeways that had been jammed through city neighborhoods and along the waterfront, the god-awful speculative building where ordinary builders did exactly what the City's Planning Code made them do. Something was wrong. Something was obviously wrong with what architects and planners had been doing for twenty-five years, and with what I had been taught to do in my education as an architect.

I had just completed three years of work as a consultant to the San Francisco Department of City Planning, helping to rewrite the housing design standards for the City's Planning Code, and I had designed and built the small project called Pacific Heights Townhouses as a demonstration of the ideas proposed for the new Planning Code. Pacific Heights Town-houses were decidedly modern dwellings, very dense and compact, with double height spaces and lots of sunlight, but they nestled comfortably amid their Victorian neighbors, which very little recent housing in the city had managed to do. I knew vaguely that this work was related in some way to that of some young European architects named Krier, who were interested in traditional cities. I had also heard that there was an urban design studio at Cornell that looked at cities in ways that were different from the scorched-earth planning by demolition that was taught at Columbia, Harvard, and other places. But I really knew very little about what anyone other than Jane Jacobs thought about how screwed-up architects were.

Then came *Collage City*. On my first reading of it, I felt like someone who had spent years on a Micronesian island listening to scratchy ukulele records suddenly finding himself in the middle of a Von Karajan performance of the Ninth Symphony. It has been said of the great events of 1942 and 1943 that the tide of battle shifted because Winston Churchill had unleashed upon the armies of the Axis nations the full fury of the English language. Never before *Collage City* had the fury of language been directed so magnificently at the failings of the modernist city and the intellectual underpinnings of its tacit theory.

For 181 pages, majestic sentence by majestic sentence, an argument is constructed that says that all my professional colleagues of my generation and I had been breathing a colorless and odorless poison gas from the moment we entered architecture school. What we had breathed in was a lethal concoction of naive utopianism, pseudoscience, historical determinism, and cockeyed populism. The results were those very urban renewal, federal highway, and public housing programs that were tearing San Francisco and every other city in the world to bits. What it seemed to be saying was that in my own little efforts of the past few years, I was not alone and armed with a peashooter, but that I had this giant with a mighty sword standing beside me.

I made the key passages of *Collage City* required reading in every course I taught. Later I added its companion book, Michael Dennis's *Court and Garden*. Michael Dennis and his college roommate Fred Koetter had been among Colin Rowe's early urban design students at Cornell and have built their powerful careers as architects and teachers on their years with Colin Rowe. I hoped that my own efforts stood on the same ground. In some ways, I felt confident in what I was doing as an architect and teacher, but I always wondered if Colin Rowe, the man whom I had appropriated to stand behind it all, would think I had gotten it right. In his eyes, would my version of city architecture be too literally contextual or not literal enough, or were the projects just too dinky to be worth considering? For twenty-two years, I did not have the chance to find out.

Then in 1999, the Seaside Institute staged an event at Seaside, Florida, in which many of the leading teachers and critics in the architectural world were invited to discuss the New Urbanist movement and the works of its principal practitioners. It was an interesting cast of characters on both sides. The New Urbanist roster included Jacqlyn Robertson, Ray Gindroz, Andres Duany, Elizabeth Plater-Zyberk, Stephanos Polysoides, Elizabeth Moule, and me. There was a longer list of stellar critics, including Robert Campbell of the *Boston Globe*, Alex Krieger of Harvard, Withold Rybcyzinski of the University of Pennsylvania, Doug Kelbaugh from Ann Arbor, Alan Jacobs, Donlyn Lyndon, and Harrison Fraker from Berkeley—and Colin Rowe. I would finally get to meet the man who had served as my appropriated mentor in absentia all these years.

Seaside is very difficult to get to. One of the routes is to fly to Fort Walton Beach, Florida, a small place in the Florida Panhandle, and take a van for about an hour and a quarter. When I arrived in Fort Walton and found my van driver, I realized that I would be sharing the van with a very old man in a wheelchair, Colin Rowe. He looked ill, wasted, and very uncomfortable, with puffy purple ankles and puffy feet with sores on them stuffed into slippers. There was a great maneuvering with canes and lots of pushing and pulling and grunting, and we finally got him seated in the front of the van. I sat behind him and observed his head poking over the back of the van seat. I realized that from inside this blotchy pink dome with its wisps of white hair had come *The Mathematics of the Ideal Villa*, *Roma Interotta*, and *Collage City*. The pyrotechnic language, the dazzling wit, the erudition, the mind with the strength of Sampson that had pushed down the intellectual pillars of the modernist city was just there, inches away, sheathed in this sweating, not very attractive flesh.

At infrequent intervals on the long, ugly ride to Seaside, I made attempts to engage him in conversation. Like other very old men, he seemed to find refuge from his multiple discomforts by swathing himself in layer upon layer of grumpiness. He responded to my conversational attempts either with total silence or with speechlike sounds that seemed to emanate from the depth of his colon, traveled through god-knows what, and emerged as BLLEEEAAAUGH or SCHLUUURRRPHG. Eventually we arrived at Seaside, and there ensued another great struggle with canes and the wheelchair, several of us grunting and pushing and pulling until he was at last seated in his chair with someone to escort him to his quarters. Then he finally spoke, in an elegant voice, free of all colonic dyspepsia. The diction was John Gielgud; the tamber of the voice was Lionel Barrymore. "This," he said grandly, "is a very strange place."

The presentations began early the next morning with Colin Rowe seated in the first row of critics in his wheelchair with his two canes. Throughout the day, he didn't say much, but when something seemed to displease him he unleashed one of his colonic eruptions. Now and then, the Gielgud/Barrymore voice would appear with a remark laced with the kind of savage bitchiness that one reserves for the laziest and most pretentious students at a school where one hopes never to be invited back. At one point in the middle of a presentation, he shouted, "C minus." When the stunned presenter said something like "Huh?" he repeated it louder, "C MINUS." At another point, he wheeled himself over to a big plan map in the middle of a presentation, rapped it loudly with one of his canes, and said, " I've *beeeen* there, to this very spot. Ghaaastly place. GHAAAASTLY!"

My turn to present came at six o'clock at the very end of the long day. What I was going to show were the three projects that were not only our most important current work but each of which in different ways represented the culmination of what I had been working toward in the twenty-two years since I had first read *Collage City*. What a situation: showing what was really a summa of my lifework to that point to friends and colleagues in front of the man whose thinking had shaped all of it— and finding him to be this foul-tempered, evil-tongued, totally intimidating wreck of a man. Of all the ten thousand forms of trepidation I had ever felt before presenting work, there had never been anything quite like this.

Partway into the presentation, Colin Rowe interrupted me as he had others all day long—only it was not the great dyspeptic bleat, nor was it the Gielgud/Barrymore voice. He said, "As Ken Frampton would say . . . ," and his voice became the gentle, erudite voice of Kenneth Frampton. Frampton, like Colin Rowe, is a man of immense learning. He speaks softly, almost in whispers, as if the act of downloading his great burden of thought causes him physical pain. The sentences were those two-hundred-word, conditional, pluperfect, subjunctive constructions of a complexity that I thought only Kenneth Frampton was capable of, and he most likely only on the third draft. The references were to the kinds of obscure things that Frampton likes to talk about: Swiss housing estates I had never heard of, Italian Rationalist revivals of seventeenth-century Spanish block plans in Naples, other things I can't remember.

It took me some time to realize that this very strange speech, muttered in a way that the transcript of the event caught none of, was intended as his oblique form of high praise. He *liked* the work. He was actually *smiling*, something I had not imagined he could do.

When it was over, I went to the bar that overlooks the beach. Colin Rowe was sitting by himself, watching the sunset, his shaking hand guiding an impatiently awaited martini to his lips. He motioned for me to join him and, what the hell, I too ordered a martini. We chatted for a while, and he was friendly and cordial. By the time we were on the second martini, I was comfortably trading gossip and architectural obscurata with the twentieth century's greatest master of those two forms of discourse.

I thought to myself that from my peculiar vantage point, martinis in the sunset with Colin Rowe is a Walter Mitty moment of the first order. It is the last mountain stage of the Tour de France. At the end of the day, with three mountain passes behind them, an unknown American is riding wheel to wheel with the invincible Miguel Indurain, up the final brutal climb to l'Alpe d'Huez. The year must be around 1995, when Big Mig was in his prime. The roar of the CNN helicopter is smothered by 150,000 chanting voices at the edge of the road: MEE-GELL, DAN-YELL, MEE-GELL, DAN-YELL. Oh God, the glory of it.

The life of an architect, like that of a bicycle racer, is not without the possibility of occasional hard-won rewards.

Black Plans

Colin Rowe died shortly after that memorable day at Seaside. The people who presented work at Seaside were all architects who had spent twenty-five years or so attempting to reform what the generation of their teachers and first employers had done in the preceding twenty-five years. All of us, including Colin Rowe, represented the fourth quarter of the twentieth century's attempt to undo much of what the third quarter had done with such vigor. All of us had begun our work independently of one another, and much later found that we had a common ground and a basis for some kind of collective action. Each of us in our own way had pieced together a version of the story of what had gone wrong with the built world in the years after World War II.

There is lots to read on the subject, and no one would say that architecture or architectural ideas alone were responsible for the fragmentation and abandonment of American cities, the failures of public housing and urban renewal, or the ghastliness of sprawl. The power of *Collage City* was that it showed us, the young architects of the 1970s, exactly how the things we were taught to do, the people we were taught by, and the ideas we had come to believe in were complicit in the mess we saw around us. Architectural ideas were by no means the whole story of the postwar city building debacle, but they were part of the story, and *Collage City* helped us to understand which part.

The argument of *Collage City* is about what modernist town planning did to cities, how and why the spaces of the postwar city are deficient, what ugliness and incoherence actually consist of, and how one makes a map of them. Once the clear and descriptive map is made, one can begin to change the map and thereby correct the deficiencies it describes.

Collage City did not provide all the answers, and for people who are not initiates into architectural debate, it is a somewhat opaque and difficult book. But for many architects and students, it provided the structure of an argument upon which to graft everything else we learned about public policy, development practice, traffic engineering, and every other subject that bears upon the building of the world. But more than anything else, it taught many of us to recognize the destructiveness and frequent silliness of the architectural object that stands defiantly or indifferently to the fabric of the city.

For those of us who did not have the good fortune to be Colin Rowe's students, *Collage City* was our introduction to the methods of analysis and drawing he evolved with his students during the years of the Cornell Urban Design Studio. One of these methods, the aerial axonometric, is a simple, mechanically constructed version of an aerial perspective, which can depict accurately the spatial qualities of a whole sector of a city. The other is an abstract method of depicting urban space, called a figure/ground drawing or a "black plan," derived from Gestalt psychology. In this method of drawing a plan, buildings are depicted as solid black, and

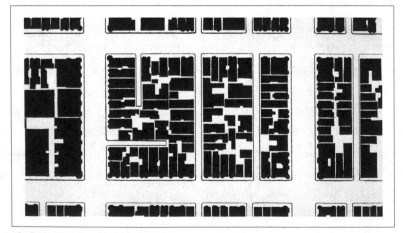

Black plan, San Francisco blocks

everything else is the white of the paper. While both of these forms of representation are tedious and time-consuming to construct, neither requires exceptional representational ability, and they open the possibility of depicting and interpreting urban space to a wide range of people who do not happen to have the drafting skill of Leonardo da Vinci (or Rob Krier).

Colin Rowe's students at Cornell, and others who have followed their methods subsequently, are like the early medieval monastery scribes who kept classical learning alive during the long, dark times of general illiteracy. The patient, detailed recording of city forms in black ink became the conservatory of a critically important body of knowledge that was nearly wiped away. That knowledge concerns the way that buildings shape the spaces of the city and the realization that urbanism is above all a spatial matter.

Le Corbusier wrote in big type as Observation 27 of *The Athens Charter,* first published in 1943:

THE ALIGNMENT OF DWELLINGS ALONG TRANSPORTATION ROUTES MUST BE PROHIBITED.

He considered the sidewalk an absurdly ineffectual protection against the "menace of death" from the automobile. Sigfried Giedion did not bother with the big typeface in *Space, Time and Architecture,* but he made up for it with language that is even more dogmatic:

> *The first necessity in the development of the future town: the abolition of the rue corridor. There is no longer any place for the street with its traffic lane running between rows of houses; it cannot possibly be permitted to persist.*

They did not mince words, these modernists. In the simplest terms, the main differences between traditional urbanism and modernist urbanism, as it is codified in *The Athens Charter* and *Space, Time and Architecture,* have to do first with the relationship between buildings and streets and second with the question of segregation versus integration of the constituent elements of the city. The modernists of CIAM (Le Corbusier, Gropius, Giedion, et al.) were absolutely clear on these subjects.

Buildings and streets each had their own separate imperatives, and the geometries and alignments of one should have nothing to do with the geometries and alignments of the other. Streets with buildings lined up along them—the normal condition in every city in the world—were not only a bad idea, but they *"must be prohibited"*; they *"cannot possibly be permitted to persist."* The uses of the city—dwelling, commerce, work, play, and civil administration—each needed its own enclave; they did not belong all mixed up with one another.

An important consequence of this modernist scheme of things was that the architects of individual buildings were liberated from obligation to anything but the building they were designing. The street, public space, the building next door were all somebody else's affair and did not impede the architect in pursuit of his muse. It is small wonder that these modernist planning doctrines would have some tenacious appeal to architects, especially considering that their very survival today, in a culture in which media and careers are so inexorably intertwined, depends upon their ability perpetually to produce forms that are novel, arresting, and newsworthy.

The liberation of the building from the street was a first, decisive step in the progressive liberation of architecture from almost everything, a liberation now celebrated with relentless regularity on the pages of the *New York Times*. Once the war of liberation starts, you never know where it will end. After the slaying of the street came the whole physical context of the city. After architecture was liberated from the history and spatial order of the city, it was liberated from the technology of its own production, because (the reasoning goes) architecture should not simply memorialize *process*. The final casualty is *program*—that is, the actual life contained within buildings and the ostensible reason people spend money to build them. In the heady, conceptual world of architectural self-reference, nothing is more banal and deliberating than the idea of utility. The Cartesian space that Le Corbusier dreamt of and Heidegger mocked is the matrix within which these liberated, ever more "conceptual" buildings float, like bits of diced fruit in Jell-O.

Figure/ground drawings or "black plans," as they are sometimes called, revealed what is wrong with Le Corbusier's propositions and the entire culture of self-referential, liberated buildings and segregated land use that emanated from them. If the severing of the geometries of buildings from the geometries of streets is an act of emancipation—perhaps a first and crucial act—then the laborious drawing of "black plans" is its opposite. Black plans are an act of grounding, a way of depicting something in relation to other things, spatially and temporally. The fascinating property of black plans is that, once you get used to studying them, they allow you to construct an entire narrative of being in a place and how that place came to be. You can project yourself inside the drawing and truly imagine the experiences it depicts.

For instance, a figure/ground drawing of New York City made at a large enough scale to see each building reveals the entire history of New York housing reform and housing legislation, from the tenements of the nineteenth century to HUD's latest initiatives to redress the postwar horrors of public housing. One can "read" from the black shapes the point at which the New Tenement Law of 1901 introduced light wells and compulsory ventilation for all rooms. Even more clearly, you can see where Title I Urban Renewal funding and eminent domain in the 1960s allowed Robert Moses's Public Housing Authority to wipe out blocks of the city and build their version of Radiant City. And one not only sees a historical narrative, one truly experiences the spaces. The difference between the street life of Lower Manhattan or Madison Avenue, or the comforting containment of Bryant Park and the terrifying, amorphous "open spaces" of Moses's projects, jumps right off the page at you.

It is well understood that *The Athens Charter* represented a decisive turning point throughout the world, that it marked the great breach in urban history that coincided with World War II. It is less well understood that the counterreformation to the ideas of *The Athens Charter*, as represented by *Collage City*, the Cornell Urban Design Studio, and the methods of urban analysis that evolved there, has also by now had its own dramatic effect.

This is most clear in the current generation of building in Berlin. Berlin's history, and the huge infusion of capital that followed reunification in 1989, set the stage for the largest and most dramatic transformation of a city since the postwar reconstructions of fifty years ago. Both the method of the reconstruction and the character of most of it could not have been conceived without the contribution of the Cornell Urban Design Studio.

The director of all of the planning and the billions of dollars of construction that has occurred in Berlin since 1989 has been Senatsbaudirektor Hans Stimmann. All of the projects that he has initiated, overseen, and directed have been shaped by an extraordinary series of maps prepared at his initiative. The most important and intriguing of these maps are black plans straight out of Cornell. The tragedies of Berlin, its incredible political history, and the physical transformations that have accompanied its various chapters are captured more compellingly and more succinctly by these maps than they could be by any other medium. It is worth becoming a reader of figure/ground drawings just to have the experience of unlocking the story of these maps.

Stimmann's figure/ground drawings, though he refers to them as "black plans," depend heavily on color. They depict all of the buildings in the city at one time in black, with the additions or demolitions of another particular time superimposed in a color. His most effective way of presenting the maps is to project them in rapid sequence in Powerpoint, so that one can see the physical city morphing before one's eyes as the historical narrative of Berlin from 1940 to 2010 unfolds.

The first map shows Berlin in 1940, with the buildings of the built city all in black. It is a dense, consistent tapestry of complex, black shapes, cut through by a web of medieval streets and by major boulevards and squares that create the settings for larger, simpler black shapes, which represent the monuments—the opera house, the museums, the Stadtkirche, the Reichstag, the Brandenburg Gate, and so on. One also sees in the middle of it all a large white space, which represents the Tiergarten of Karl Josef Linie, one of the finest of all urban parks. This is the capital of Prussia as it was built by the Hohenzollern kings and minimally altered in the first four decades of the twentieth century. The patterns of the map are not unlike the patterns of the historic centers of Paris, London, or Vienna today.

Superimposed on the black pattern of the 1940 city in light red cross-hatching are the proposed but never realized interventions of the National Socialists. The classical geometries of the Albert Speer plan are not unlike those of the earlier monuments, but they are at ten times the scale and they cut ruthlessly and arbitrarily through the patterns of the black ink. One sees clearly why Speer needed to expropriate seventy-five thousand "Jew apartments" to relocate the Aryan Berliners who would be displaced by his dream. Figure/ground drawings by themselves do not teach you the history of the city, but they validate and clarify what one may dimly understand more vividly than any other medium.

The next map in the series shows in black what remained of the 1940 city in 1945, with the buildings destroyed in the war colored purple. As one would expect from every photograph and newsreel one has ever seen of Berlin at the end of the war, there is lots of purple. There are, however, a surprising number of black shapes remaining, even in the center of the city, where the greatest concentration of large monuments were clustered. The next map shows the city in 1953, with the war damage removed and lots of new white space.

The next map is a shocker. It depicts demolitions between 1953 and 1989 in dark blue, with whatever remained from 1953 to 1989 in black. This time most of the buildings are blue. In both East and West Berlin, there are more colored buildings than in the map of 1945. Between 1953 and 1989, town planners in both parts of the city, serving competing economic philosophies and political regimes, each destroyed *more of historic Berlin within their jurisdictions than did World War II.*

In 1935 Le Corbusier pronounced, "New cities will replace old cities." Perhaps it is not surprising that modernist planners, whose Koran was *The Athens Charter,* chose Berlin to unleash their most merciless attack on the historic city. Surely, there is no place that the city of the *ancien régime* could be associated with history more odious than that of Berlin, and the actions of postwar planners have the character of a Jihad. Even slightly damaged buildings, buildings by the greatest masters, buildings that had served benign purposes—such as Karl Friedrich Schinkel's Academy of Fine Arts, which was all of the above—were not spared in the frenzy. What occurred even exceeded the fervor with which the communist regime ravaged the monuments and the historic fabric of the once glorious city of Beijing after 1949.

The book and exhibition of Stimmann's maps also contain extraordinary, heartrending photographs. Sets of three pictures show the same

Berlinerstadtschloss, 1930

Berlinerstadtschloss, 1945

Berlinerstadtschloss site, 1995

places in Berlin in the 1920s or 1930s, the 1950s or 1960s, and the 1980s or 1990s. The first images of each set depict the city fabric, public spaces, and monuments of a great European capital, exactly the sorts of places that today constitute the cherished and meticulously preserved historic centers of other European capitals—Prague, Paris, London. The 1950s and 1960s photographs confirm what the 1945 figure/ground map shows: that the historic city was largely intact after the war, battered but definitely not destroyed, and fully restorable. It is the last photograph of each set that makes you want to weep. They show neither the old capital, its buildings, and public spaces. Nor do they show a shining new vision of a modernist Radiant City. Mostly there are pictures of parking lots—parking lots and big roadways, with a disjointed scattering of modern buildings of such crashing banality that one thinks not of a European city layered with the culture of centuries but of someplace out near the airport outside of Burbank or Cincinnati. One does not have to know a lot about the twentieth century to have an understanding of the reasons for modernist hostility to historic Berlin, but that understanding does not diminish the magnitude of its tragedy. Klaus von Choltitz, the Wehrmacht general who refused to obey Hitler's order to burn Paris, is considered a hero, but the postwar planners of East and West Berlin did to their own city exactly what von Choltitz refused to do to Paris.

Berlin new construction, 1953–89

The next drawing in the series shows what little was left standing in 1989 in black and the new construction of the years 1953 to 1989 in orange (here shown as gray). Two things are striking about this map. First, there is no way to tell where the boundary is between East and West Berlin, because all of the orange shapes are more or less alike. Second, one sees that all of the orange shapes are completely different from the black ones. The new kinds of buildings in the East are indistinguishable from those in the West. This is truly the triumph of the *Zeitgeisters*, the spirit of the times obliterating the most extreme political and economic differences.

What is so different about the later orange shapes and the earlier black ones is the way they interact with the white of the page. In the black parts of the map, the white parts are usually *contained* by black shapes, and the white parts form recognizable shapes of their own. One can see and imagine walking through streets, courtyards, public squares, and so on. In the colored parts of the map, however, the white is just the white of the page, a background for the colored shapes, but it never takes on a shape itself. You can't tell from the drawing what the white part is. This is the genius of the figure/ground drawing. It shows in the clearest possible way the difference between the vacuous, formless nonspaces of the modernist city, with its "liberated," self-referential buildings, and the formed and contained public spaces of the traditional city, in which buildings and public space—black shapes and the white of the page—engage in a complex, mutually interdependent interaction.

The difference between the older black shapes and the newer orange ones represents nothing less than a revolution. I had my own whiff of the intoxication that accompanied the erasing of black and white shapes and replacing them with free floating colored ones in the years 1953 to 1989. As a nineteen-year-old with the first inklings of an interest in architecture, I first visited Berlin in 1959, and several things about that journey remain as vivid memories.

The first and most striking thing one saw was how much more effectively the Western powers were at using Berlin as a propaganda tool than the Soviet Union was. To a young student, West Berlin in 1959 was incredible fun. It had been injected with all the financial juices of the Marshall Plan and then the *Wirtschaftswunder* (economic miracle) of the 1950s, and it was absolutely jumping at all hours of the day and night. People, especially young ones, looked cool as could be. East Berlin, by contrast, was by far the grimmest place I had ever seen. On most blocks, the rubble of the war had not even been swept away. People (including the young ones) looked terrible, and the food was scarce and inedible. The making of the orange shapes on the map was well under way in West Berlin, with lots of construction sites and cranes everywhere, but in the East the orange shapes all came later.

I saw only one major construction project in progress in East Berlin in 1959. It was called Stalin Allee, later renamed Karl Marx Allee, and to a young student breathing the intoxicating ethers of modernism, it was a complete absurdity, particularly compared to what was going on in the West. Stalin Allee was then several blocks of heavy-handed Soviet-style, neo-classical facade emerging amid the rubble like a giant movie set with nothing behind it. No buildings, only this monumental facade. The fact that this process of building civic facades first and filling in with buildings behind them later was more or less the way that large sections of Paris, London, and Vienna had been built was completely lost on this nineteen-year-old. To me and to most others, it was clear that the new West Berlin was free, bright, and real, and that the new East Berlin was totalitarian, drab, and fake. The Cold War seemed like no contest.

But long before the political and economic structure of the East crumbled before the might of Western capitalism, the urbanistic sensibilities that produced Stalin Allee collapsed in their confrontation with modernism. The hegemony of modern architecture East and West long preceded the destruction of the Berlin Wall.

For me in 1959, the freest, most real, and brightest of the new buildings in West Berlin—one of the images that stirred in me the dream of being an architect—was the Kongresshalle, a swoopy, zoomy thing made of gravity-defying, thin concrete by Boston architect Hugh Stubbins. In the end gravity won out, and the Kongresshalle eventually suffered a major structural failure, but in 1959 it stood across an empty field, facing the burnt hulk of Schinkel's Reichstag in East Berlin, as a shining promise of modernity amid the politically contaminated ruins of antiquity.

And there were more promises nearby. In 1957, the giants of CIAM—Le Corbusier himself, Gropius, Mies van der Rohe, Alvar Aalto, Oscar Niemeyer, and others—built the Hansa Viertel, an exposition of new housing that borrowed the surroundings of Linie's magnificent Tiergarten and therefore really were towers in a park. The Hansa Viertel seemed quite OK in a bland sort of way and gave no inkling of the soul-numbing landscape of parking lots, motorways, and isolated mid-rise clunkers that were about to engulf the city.

It all came soon enough, and soon enough people began to understand the emptiness of the promise. *Collage City* was published in 1977, and by the early 1980s there were architects who well understood the depth of its criticism of almost everything that had been built in European cities since the war. Berlin was then in the early planning stages of the International Bauausstellung scheduled for 1987, which, like the Berlin housing expositions of 1927 and 1957, would showcase the latest thinking and best architects in the realm of urban housing. One architect who had digested *Collage City* and the earlier poetic writings of Aldo Rossi about the lost memory of the European city was the influential, eloquent professor and practitioner Josef Paul Kleiheus. Kleiheus had access to the editorial pages of the *Berliner Morgenpost,* a paper of equivalent stature to the *New York Times*, and he wrote a passionate series of articles critical of the early planning for the 1987 exposition. The articles lamented the current plight of cities and proposed a polemic for the 1987 exposition as a step toward the recovery of the heritage of European urbanism. As a direct result of this series of editorials, Kleiheus was made director of the International Bauausstellung of 1987, or IBA, as it came to be known.

Kleiheus coined the term "critical reconstruction" as the theoretical underpinning of IBA, and it is a term and a set of ideas that have been carried forward continually since that time by Stimmann and his colleagues. Neither Kleiheus nor Stimmann has ever proposed anything like the overt revivalism of Karl Marx Allee, and neither has ever rejected modern architecture. What they have rejected is the modernist planning idea of the isolated, self-referential building as it is revealed by figure/ground drawings in the manner of Colin Rowe's students. They recognized that cities consist of spaces *contained* by buildings, and they rejected *The Athens Charter*'s dissociation of buildings from streets and its segregation of uses by zones.

The projects of IBA, and more dramatically those executed during Stimmann's tenure, show that modern architecture stripped of its lunatic planning ideology can provide the building blocks for the reconstruction of the space of the city as it existed from antiquity until the hubristic madness of the postwar era. Stimmann works regularly with the brightest stars of the architectural world, and he respects and trusts them, but only to a point. He trusts them to make fine and interesting buildings, but he does not trust them to make the ground plan of the city. That ground plan is the last of his series of black plans, a figure/ground drawing of the city as it will exist in 2010. Stimmann learned his lessons from Colin Rowe, and he knows that not all architects, not even all very talented and famous architects, have learned that same lesson. He therefore imposes on his architects a ground plan in which the black shapes of buildings define and give form to the white shapes between them, in more or less the same way as the black shapes of the 1940 map do.

The big interventions that Stimmann has directed prove finally and conclusively that modern buildings, even highly inventive and assertive modern buildings, can make urban spaces with the same definition, clarity, and quality that the public spaces of great cities have always had.

Sometimes, the great architects seem about as comfortable within the *dictat* of the black plans as hyperactive five-year-olds lined up at their little desks in the classroom of the strictest teacher. The great architects may fidget, but they all more or less behave themselves. Even at Potsdamer Platz, where the full might of global corporate capitalism sponsored architectural superstardom in a titanic battle of egos, the zoots and slashes of late modernist formalism whir around harmlessly inside coherent street walls and alongside a handsomely shaped series of large and small public courtyards and squares. When there is a big event at Potsdamer Platz, such as the Berlin Film Festival, with the courts and squares jammed with people, it is clear beyond a doubt that both the need for and the possibility of constructing real, living, urban public space did not die with the Beaux Arts.

Stimmann and his staff have enough understanding of how buildings work—floor plate sizes, daylighting requirements, fire exiting, and the like—to have created an urban ground plan that makes both workable buildings and coherent public spaces. For the most part, the black plans have given architects guidance where they need it and allowed them to do their own thing otherwise, usually without major conflict.

A notable exception was the design phase of Frank Gehry's Deutsche Genossenschaft Bank, next to the Brandenburg Gate on Pariser Platz, one of the most important historic places in the city. The urban design for the reconstruction of the square and the design guidelines for new buildings to redefine its edges were originally proposed by Kleiheus, who also won the commission to build two exquisite little neo-classical pavilions, replacing two destroyed Schinkel buildings immediately flanking the gate itself. The bank site faces the square, at right angles to the first of the Kleiheus pavilions.

Frank Gehry and the bank directors showed up at Stimmann's office with a scheme that was typical Gehry—wiggling and boogying all over the site, like his Experimental Music Project in Seattle or dozens of his other signature buildings around the world. Stimmann, who is a big imposing man, had the authority and the personal stature to tell the Pritzker

Prize architect and his powerhouse client something to the effect that the state of disrobe that may be appropriate at Venice Beach was not the level of civic propriety demanded at Pariser Platz—no way, baby—and Mr. Gehry should go back and study his Schinkel.

Amazingly, Frank Gehry did just that and produced what may be his finest and most mature, if not his most sensational, work. Facing Pariser Platz is a deeply articulated, beautifully proportioned and crafted travertine facade, with large voids of undivided glass set into the travertine. The debt to Schinkel is implicit but not overt, and this calm, monumental facade is clearly that of a modern building. One passes through the thick facade into a vestibule of similar character, and then into an amazing space. The shell of the space is a great void surrounded by office galleries, like the interior of Frank Lloyd Wright's Larkin Building, but here exquisitely detailed in warm wood paneling. Inside the void and filling its lower levels is a Frank Gehry creature, a giant fish or whale, made with incredible computer craft and housing a conference center. The back of the building is as aformal as the front is formal and crumbles into the jumble of building backs and midblocks away from the square. It is probably the most interesting and beautiful single building of the Stimmann regime.

This brilliant resolution of the tension between Stimmann and Gehry is what Colin Rowe had in mind through all those years of teaching at Cornell, and it is what *Collage City* is about. The city does not choke the architect's muse, but neither do architects run amok, like the crazed musicians who rebel against the conductor, throw down their instruments, and wreck the symphony hall in Federico Fellini's ignored masterpiece *Orchestra Rehearsal*. Fellini made *Orchestra Rehearsal* in 1980, almost at the end of his career. In its poignant ending, the musicians return to the wreckage, salvage their battered instruments, and begin, haltingly, to play again. It is where Fellini saw the world at the end of his life. If he knew about them, Fellini would have liked black plans, because like the conductor's baton, they are useful and necessary tools for the continuity of civilization.

Style

The movement called New Urbanism had its origin in the initiative of a group of architects, all of us with active or recent ties to academia. Curiously, this movement since its inception has found its staunchest resistance, its most trenchant criticism, and its most demeaning caricature in schools of architecture. Sometimes it seems that everybody welcomes the New Urbanist proposition more openly than our closest colleagues. It is easier by far to interest public housing officials and their tenants, planners, developers, politicians, bankers, even traffic engineers in the cause of New Urbanism than it is to engage architecture faculty or their students.

There is a reason for this. The mission of architectural academy is generally thought of, explicitly or implicitly, as a phenomenon related to time—the tenor of the times. It is what the Zeitgeist ethic in the architectural histories we grew up with told us, from Giedion's *Space, Time and Architecture* in 1941 to Reyner Banham's *Theory and Design in the First Machine Age* in 1960, style is linked to time, and the primary cultural problem of design is giving expression to the dominant technologies of the time. All these years later, these same ideas about time and style still dominate the education or, perhaps one should say, the indoctrination of architects.

Colin Rowe spent much of his life writing about this missionary zeal about time, and the people of my generation who were shaped directly or indirectly by the aura of his teaching know his litany. It is the architect in his role as the future's messenger that leads to the triumph of the timely over the timeless. It is the Zeitgeisters marching to the drumbeat of Hegelian dialectics that trample the fabric of the traditional city. And there is object fixation, all the reasons from the dawn of the modern movement that root modern architecture in the making of *things* as opposed to *places* and favor disengagement of those things from what is around them. To this, we must add the star system and media-based careers that are intertwined with the great power of photography to decontextualize architecture as effectively and much more perniciously than the white wall of the gallery decontextualizes art. In the photographer's studio, what architecture does to the city around it is the subject of cropping.

The antipathy between the academy and New Urbanism comes from the refusal of New Urbanists to accept the eternal quest for temporal expression as an issue of any remaining importance. The willingness of New Urbanists to use architectural style, in some cases even—dare one say it—historical styles, as a weapon in the struggle against the dreadful tide of homogenization of places is an affront to the fundamental ethos of orthodox modernism, which is still rooted in a condition that long ago ceased to exist.

At least since its introduction to the United States in the 1930s, orthodox modern architecture has had a weird and hypocritical relationship to the concept of style. Among the seminal events in the story of modern architecture in America were the 1932 Museum of Modern Art show *Modern Architecture: International Exhibition*, the accompanying book entitled *The International Style*, and the appointment of Walter Gropius as chair of the Department of Architecture at Harvard in 1937. Much of Gropius's own work formed the core of the museum exhibition and book by Henry Russell-Hitchcock and Phillip Johnson. It is significant that Gropius did not like the formalist emphasis of the exhibition and the book, and most of all he detested the term "International Style." The "International" part was OK, but "Style" (especially when capitalized) was a concept completely anathema to his conception of the modern.

Modern architecture to Gropius was a purely positivistic operation, nothing more or less than the systematic application of scientific method to the problem of habitat. Style had nothing to do with it. If a Harvard architectural student in the 1940s, 1950s, or 1960s were to design a building that was not a grouping of flat-roofed, eaveless boxes with strips of ribbon windows, he would have been told, not that he had violated a stylistic canon, but that he had failed to understand the social and technological imperatives of the times. The tension between architecture and urbanism would not now be so acute if the architectural academy had been able to sustain this original hypocrisy and simply operate as if a stable canon of design were rooted in some mysterious essence of the times. Then there might be more places like Vancouver or parts of Tel Aviv, where a consistent urban fabric is built over time out of a decidedly modernist language of architecture. But, despite the efforts of some of the best modernists, that is not what happened.

The combined effects of the denial of style (architecture is *truth*) and the harsh realities of media culture have precluded the possibility of a stable canon. The most meteoric architectural careers are based upon a particular form of nimbleness—that is, the ability to produce work that simultaneously is *news* and *truth*. The combination of both phenomena is essential. For the publication and exhibition opportunities that careers depend upon, the news part is crucial but by itself insufficient; it has to be news about social and technological imperatives. This means that the social and technological imperatives of the age have to change all the time. Of course, not all architects are adept at coining new imperatives as the occasion demands, and an important function that the media serve is to transmit newly minted imperatives of the times from their discoverers to their awaiting legions of acolytes. Since building technology and social conditions do not change rapidly enough to keep up with media culture's demand for news, new architectural imperatives have to come from extrinsic sources farther and farther afield—linguistics, poststructuralism, airplane design software, feminist literary criticism, global consumerism, and so on. Soon, architectural discourse will require its own channel, like C-SPAN, where tenure candidates and others whose livelihood is involved can keep abreast of fast-breaking events in the realm of Zeitgeist imperatives.

To be fair, it must be said that there is resistance to all of this within the modernist establishment. Some of the world's most celebrated modernists have chosen to act as if the original canons of modernism were as true and stable as they claimed to be. Richard Meier's relentless excellence assumes that the formal language of Le Corbusier is an inexhaustible and sufficient resource for whatever comes along. Switzerland's Herzog and DeMeuron treat the architecture of Mies van der Rohe in somewhat the same way. There is nothing wrong at all with this kind of supremely refined, revivalist architecture, except the absurdity of its denial to be what it is. Just talk to some of the subcontractors for Meier's Getty Museum about how hard and demanding it was to build, about how much every detail cost, and then make some claims about the technological imperatives it is based upon. The refinement of Meier's architecture is anything but the automatic by-product of the technology of the times.

Since the hegemony of mainstream modernism, there have been two fiercely held ideas about style: first, that it doesn't exist; second, that it is inexorably linked to time. Both of these ideas have crippled architects' ability to respond stylistically to the demands of place, which is in fact specifically what people most frequently hire architects to do. This divergence of view causes most pedigreed architects to think of much of their potential source of patronage as hopelessly philistine and kitsch, and it causes significant segments of society to run as far and as fast from pedigreed architects as it possibly can.

It is possible to accept the existence of style in a way that it is not in fact a phenomenon related to time. I think it was no less than Diana Vreeland, the legendary editor of *Vogue* and *Harper's Bazaar,* who made the distinction between style and fashion, claiming that style, unlike fashion, has a timeless component to it and that the truly stylish are frequently somewhat indifferent to fashion. Style, in fact, can be all sorts of things. It can be related to place, as in the buildings of Charleston; related to time, as in Art Deco; or personological, like Frank Gehry's style or Picasso's.

In the nineteenth century and the first third of the twentieth century, the architectural world's concept of style was a bit more like Diana Vreeland's and less like the Zeitgeist ideologues of today's academy. One sees this phenomenon clearly in Northern California. From the late 1890s until the end of the 1920s, the public institutions of Northern California were built for the most part by a small group of immensely gifted and superbly well-trained architects, educated at the Ecole des Beaux Arts. For the whole of their prolific careers, this little group, which included Bernard Maybeck, John Galen Howard, Willis Polk, Arthur Brown, and Julia Morgan, built a world that was in urbanistic terms a very satisfactory place. They built city fabric, public monuments, rural retreats, grand campus plans, and retail streets of great vitality, and they did it all without any theory to speak of (they were too busy for theories), but with virtuoso skill, unabashed eclecticism, and a complete absence of Zeitgeist hang-ups and ideological proscriptions. Julia Morgan had no problem at all leaping from Renaissance Florence as a source for the Fairmont Hotel on top of Nob Hill in San Francisco to rustic timber vernacular for the Ahwahnee in Yosemite. It was exactly because this eclectic skill was considered so out of date after World War II that she was denied all further opportunity to build.

Unlike Gropius and his generations of progeny, Julia Morgan's contemporaries did not pretend that style did not exist or that it was a bad word denoting a bad thing, like *masturbation*. The Gropius dogma had effects not unlike those of the Cultural Revolution in China, another instance of crazy pieties run amok. Architects systematically unlearned how to do architecture. For forty years, there has hardly been an architect alive with a fraction of the sheer skill of Arthur Brown or Julia Morgan. Drawing, detailing, building, site work and garden design, solving problems in plan, understanding how architects throughout history had done these same things—practically no contemporary architects come close to them. They were masters of style and, to a lesser degree, inventors of style, and they used whatever was stylistically appropriate for what and where they were building.

Architects who love cities can rummage through the history of architecture to find times and places like Northern California in the 1920s, when time and place were not adversaries, when architecture motivated by the stirrings of the new was built in the service of the city. One doesn't have to go far to find architecture of this kind. Certainly, a little of it is being produced right now, and some was produced throughout what we must now call the last century, but as a general convention you have only to go back to the first two decades of the twentieth century worldwide, to the generation that Nicholas Pevsner referred to as the "premoderns." There you can find an abundance of architecture that might serve as a model for those who think that place making is the most important thing that architects have to do these days. Otto Wagner in Vienna, Gunnar Asplund in Stockholm, Eliel Saarinen (not Eero) in Finland and then in the United States, Puig and Domenic in Barcelona (more than the hyper-mannerist Gaudi), Placnik in Lubiana, Berlage in Amsterdam, Sullivan in Chicago, Maybeck in Berkeley—the list of master stylists and place makers is easy to write.

In considering this list, it is interesting to note that Eleil Saarinen's magnificent and timeless Cranebrook campus was where young Wu Liangyong went to study in 1951. Eero Saarinen, Eleil's gifted son, had a meteoric career producing spectacular modernist monuments until he died in 1961 at age fifty-one. For the most part, Eero Saarinen's flashy works have not stood the test of time and now look as dated as the cars of the 1950s. It is Professor Wu who is the true spiritual heir to Eliel Saarinen.

What Professor Wu learned from his great mentor is what all architects should learn from the so-called premoderns. It is a concept of style and a mastery of styles that allowed them to be interested in the new, but not obsessively, and interested in the past, but not slavishly. It was a concept of style that never produced a dogma more important to them than the places in which they built. Architecture in the service of place demands stylistic literacy that was all but banished from architectural education as anachronistic, just as all classical Chinese learning was denounced as feudal during the Cultural Revolution. We, too, are now faced with repairing the damage caused by an ideology of unlearning.

Why the City Is Not a Work of Art

Architects, geographers, and others who worry about the phenomenon of "loss of place" could hardly have a more distinguished philosophical pedigree, extending from Kenneth Frampton backward to his adopted mentor, Hannah Arendt, to her mentor and paramour, Martin Heidegger. The line of thought that extends from Heidegger forward has had many partisans who identify loss of place as a worldwide psychological and cultural crises.

Loss of place operates both at large scale and at small scale—at the scale of the city and at the scale of the room. We've all been in thousands of placeless places, placeless buildings, placeless rooms. We spend half our lives in the same placeless room—air-conditioned so that the relationship between location and climate is severed, minimally day-lit so that time is obliterated, sealed from sounds of the outdoors (there could be birds or gun shots—it doesn't matter), washed in uniform fluorescent light so that the subscale of light and shadow within the room is washed away and the color of the light is cool, so that the particular properties of different materials mush together. It has the Pella folding partitions that subdivide hotel conference rooms or middle school cafetoriums, made so that a featureless room can adapt to different uses without being shaped by any of them. It has an Armstrong acoustic tile ceiling, featureless in itself, concealing the tactile presence of structure and mechanical systems and further muffling the sound. And it all smells like carpet glue.

Kenneth Frampton sees this featureless, bad-smelling room in which we all have spent so much time as the inevitable result of optimized production and distribution of products—the hyperefficiencies of Taylorism run rampant on a global scale. He casts the architect in the role of cultural warrior locked in combat with the producers of acoustic tile, a position that in some ways is both heroic and sustainable. The few battles that the cultural warriors actually win are so celebrated and well publicized that enlistment rates for young warriors remain high. However, it is the inherent limitations of this position combined with its attractiveness that are at the crux of the problem of the architect and the city.

Frampton makes a careful and elaborate distinction between "architecture as a critical act" and "building as a banal, almost metabolic activity." In this, he follows Hannah Arendt's distinction between work and labor: work as the product of human intelligence, labor as that of the "animal laborians." This distinction, which is at the heart of the goings-on in schools of architecture, maintains the architect's connection with the artist and architecture's identification with the avant-garde.

The perennial condition of modern art is that it stands apart from the normative and is critical of the normative. Because the placeless room we have all been in is the normative product of rationalized production, the making of a "placed" as opposed to a "placeless" room is a "critical" act. This special kind of room can be considered a work of art, because it falls within the avant-gardist ethic that has paradoxically become orthodoxy in the architectural academy. Mainstream modern architects can embrace the program of making nice rooms; that is not usually a crisis of conscience for them. To do this, they must temporarily suspend their belief in the portions of the modernist canon that reject anything so static as a room, the ideas of *plan libre* and the *promenade architectural*—modernism's perpetual journey on the road to nowhere. According to the *dictat* of these portions of the canon (again, we thank Le Corbusier), movement is glorified, stasis scorned, and the plan and cross section of a house become small versions of those of a freeway interchange. There is more to say on this subject, but for now the idea introduced here is that the value system that underlies most architectural aspiration encourages architects to be interested in the way rooms and buildings are made at the same time that it discourages them from interest in the ways that neighborhoods and towns are made.

An essential part of the critical work of art is its frame, the boundary that separates it from the rest of the world. For Frampton, a bounded domain is an absolute precondition for "an architecture of resistance." Only the "bounded place/form" will stand up to the "processal flux of the megalopolis." Frampton's writings are filled with amazing phraseology, but "processal flux" stands as my personal favorite. These are the terms with which Frampton, in his *Studies in Tectonic Culture*, revisited the works of Louis Kahn and followed Kahn from his grand proposals for Philadelphia through the architecture of his late years. Kahn eventually gave up on the city, or lost interest under the press of architectural commissions, and Frampton does the same, either because place making at the scale of the city is too hard or, more importantly, because city making is not "critical" because it is not "bounded."

For Heidegger, the crisis he called "loss of nearness" was partially the nearness of the phenomenal world—light, sound, tactility, time. But it was also fundamentally the loss of nearness to other people. The city, as Richard Sennett has so eloquently written, is the unbounded experience of otherness. The boundary that prevents passage of the unexpected, unknown *other* is what distinguishes the noncity from the city, the shopping mall from the street. It distinguishes the global automobile suburb in its late-twentieth-century form from Paris, London, New York, or Alexandria, Virginia. Cities and parts of cities don't have frames around them, and they are not mounted on the decontextualizing white walls of the gallery. In the privatized noncity of boundaries, we are protected from the unexpected other, but in the city we are connected to him and vulnerable to his presence. In the city the essential condition is connection, not boundary—direct proximity to the unknown and unknowable. It is why the street is inherently exhilarating, didactic, and dangerous in ways that the shopping mall cannot be.

The city, however, cannot be "critical" in the same sense as a building or a room. It is not only without boundary, but by its very size and by the economics of the processes involved in its making, it is necessarily the product of normative production, the labor of the animal laborians.

City makers cannot refuse normative materials and normative construction techniques and still hope to make town fabric. If you think you can build housing on a large scale and never use textured drywall, good luck. Many of us can agree that our collective intent should be to resist the production of the soulless, placeless, history-less, plastic world of the late twentieth century, to replace it at all scales with Heideggerian "nearness." Our dilemma, then, is this: the strategy for making places that accomplish this end at the scale of rooms and buildings is fundamentally in conflict with strategies that do the same thing at the scale of neighborhoods and towns. Cities and parts of cities are inherently unbounded and are by necessity made in normative ways, unlike works of art.

We architects have a deep, perplexing dilemma, not an esoteric or purely theoretical dilemma, but one that throws us into conflict every working day—about which jobs to take and which to avoid; about how to write contracts and how to do working drawings; about material selection, the writing of specifications, and the thousands of daily decisions while buildings are being made. Vinyl siding is dreadful stuff, no question about it. It looks all right from a distance, but up close you can see that it is fake wood; it feels and smells awful, and environmentally it couldn't be worse. On the other hand, integrating the poor into the mainstream of society is a good idea. If one sets out to make a new street on which people have the experience of city life in all its complexity and otherness—old people, young people, poor ones, not poor ones, different races mixed together—one finds oneself very rapidly in the realm of vinyl siding.

The reasons that low-income housing just has to be clad in vinyl siding or something no better are inescapable: cost, maintenance, durability, and the important fact that it take almost no skill to install. So what are the choices? Design low-income housing that will never be built (society is not good enough for what I have to offer); avoid the subject altogether (the usual strategy for people with architectural pretensions); or somehow find a way to come to terms with vinyl siding. This is where architects and town builders come face to face with the Alice Waters/Julia Child conflict: try to restructure the world or act critically and strategically within a society one cannot completely remake.

Since the middle of the nineteenth century, there have been successive, failed attempts to create a seamless design ethos that united the work of artisans, architects, and town builders. The various incarnations of the Arts and Crafts movement around the world all had the goal of a unified, egalitarian ethic of design that operated at the scale of kitchen utensils, at the scale of city-regions, and at every scale in between.

These attempts all fell short of their goal, in the same way and for the same reasons. The industrialized grandchild of the Arts and Crafts movement, the Bauhaus, and the architecture now championed by Kenneth Frampton have had a similar fate. All of them, from the moment of their conception, were *doomed to be chic*. The career of William Morris, Marxist, member of the Fabian Society, spiritual leader of the Arts and Crafts, sums it all up. His furniture designs and textiles were intended as artifacts accessible to all and expressing the dignity of the workers involved in their production. It is an unfortunate but inescapable fact that the integrity of material and craft in these objects, not to mention the dignity of the workers producing them, costs so very much that William Morris's furniture and textiles quickly became emblems for only the richest of the Fabian socialists—radical chic in its original form. The same is true of Bauhaus artifacts. Just check out the price list for Mies van der Rohe chairs.

The genius of the Model T was that the workers who made it could afford to own it, and it thereby transformed producers into consumers. The products of the Arts and Crafts, and all the objects and architecture that emanate from Arts and Crafts values to this day, have never achieved the self-perpetuating character of the Model T. This is a problem that permeates the macroeconomics of globalization, as manufacturers chase after ever-receding labor markets whose workers *can't yet* afford to be consumers of what they make.

It is appropriate that the design of Alice Waters's restaurant Chez Panisse is a lovely work of Arts and Crafts revival, because everything about the place is completely steeped in the spirit of William Morris. Both the enduring power of his ideas and their inherent limitations are embodied in the gorgeous curvy redwood and glass front door to the restaurant, the design of which, according to a probably apocryphal local legend, was the product of a *two-week* retreat conducted by Alice and Berkeley architectural guru Christopher Alexander. There is nothing wrong with the door, quite the contrary; the question is, can one remake the world one two-week door at a time?

The architecture of Frampton's cultural warriors has, for the most part, a similar trajectory to Mies's chairs and the Chez Panisse door. There can be no denying the splendid qualities of the architecture that he celebrates and promotes. From the works of Louis Kahn and Luis Barrigan in the 1960s to those of Alvaro Siza and Raphael Moneo in the 1990s, these buildings show us that phenomenological "nearness" can exist in the modern world and be constructed by modern means. He has quite brilliantly articulated a design ethos as a counterstrategy to plastic soullessness, but it only really works for elite buildings and elite artifacts. It is a repeat of the design strategies of the Arts and Crafts and the Bauhaus, which were in fundamental contradiction to their ostensible social agenda. It can never really address cheap, normative buildings or the fabric of the city. The city has ceased to interest him because he recognizes it as the stuff of the animal laborians, and in this he has carried most of the architectural academy, the architectural press, and the museum establishment with him. In the cultural world that revolves around architecture, the pervasiveness of Kenneth Frampton's ideas and way of thinking is almost total.

It is no coincidence that the various branches of the Arts and Crafts movement have more than their share of holy martyrs and tragic biographies, great figures whose lives ended badly because practically no one could afford the things they made so exquisitely: William Morris, Charles Rennie Mackintosh, Charles and Henry Greene. The story of the Greene brothers, the great builders of wooden bungalows in Pasadena, whose working lives effectively ended almost twenty-five years before their deaths, is particularly poignant. They were the principal protagonists in the story of the California bungalow, a house type that comes closest to bridging the chasm between Framptonian tectonics and city building. Greene and Greene and their dozen or so exquisite buildings were canonized by architectural historians Esther McCoy, David Gebhardt, and Vincent Scully. Only in Japan, and there only in sacred shrines and palaces, has the craft of assembling wooden buildings ever achieved such refinement.

But it was two other Pasadena brothers, Arthur and Alfred Heineman, along with anonymous others, who accomplished what the Greenes refused to do or had no interest in: translating the bungalow aesthetic into a way of building that produced whole streets and neighborhoods, affordable to most and buildable by people of modest ability. Through pattern books and such publications as *The American Craftsman* and *Bungalow Magazine*, the Craftsman bungalow became a conventional way of building for a generation. It was a simple frame house with a robust timber porch that did not tax the skill of most carpenters. The porches usually faced a narrow, tree-lined street, and cars were tucked away on the back of the lot. One must ask whether thousands of beautiful streets and many of the most graceful, enduring, and beloved sections of cities and towns throughout North America are an achievement at least comparable to those dozen exquisitely crafted buildings by Greene and Greene.

Perhaps the most intelligent framer of questions of this kind was Berkeley's great architectural historian, Spiro Kostoff, who died tragically at age fifty-five, just as the force of his contribution was beginning to be felt outside the immediate circle of his students and colleagues. Before Kostoff, architectural history from the very beginnings of the subject was a subspecies of art history, focused on formal issues and great works. Kostoff challenged that historiography and fundamentally recast the discipline as a branch of social history. Kostoff loved architecture and great works, but he placed them not in a picture frame on a white wall, but in a great unfolding panorama of civilization. One of the main pleasures of teaching at Berkeley was sneaking the time now and then to sit in on Kostoff's majestic lectures. Architectural works were not paintings in a gallery or specimens in a bottle. In Kostoff's cosmology, Frampton's "bounded place/form" had no meaning, because it is the city—the whole, messy, complex, unbounded city—that is the stage upon which the drama of architecture is performed.

Another Truth

The previous essays have argued that architects, as the products of architectural education, have something in common with people who were educated in creationism. Creationists know vaguely that there is such a thing as evolution, that there is evidence to support it, and that most other people believe in it. But with architects, it is not evolution that is a forbidden and never whispered idea—it is the concept of style. For about sixty-five years, since the hegemony of Walter Gropius at Harvard, architects everywhere have been taught that style does not exist or that, if it exists, it applies to other things and not to their lifework. They know that their subject is concerned with *truth*, not with style. There are several forms of truth—in fact, there are new ones all the time—but the most popular and pervasive one has to do with *tectonics*, what one builds from and how these materials are assembled. If one builds out of good, solid stuff, and if one can see in the end how it all went together and what holds up what, then one has built something with *integrity*, something that is or conveys the truth. That is what most architects try to do, and they know that it is very important, because tectonic integrity is one of the qualities so lacking in that ubiquitous, placeless, featureless room that nobody likes.

Unfortunately for them, however, these architects are immediately confronted with hostile, fiercely held beliefs as soon as they pass through the walls of the architectural compound. Those few who actually attempt to build the normal fabric of the city, particularly its housing, are immediately brought before the Tribunal of the Grand Inquisitors. There are three Grand Inquisitors: the Director of Marketing, the Chief Building Inspector in charge of code enforcement, and the Value Engineer. All three despise the idea of tectonic integrity, and together they are vested with the authority to insure that there is never a trace of it in normal city buildings, especially housing.

The Director of Marketing sells things, and what he knows how to sell are known and knowable commodities. That is where style comes in. Truth is just too vague a concept for him; he needs something tangible, like *Spanish*.

The Chief Building Inspector protects things, especially from fires. What protects simple, inexpensive building materials from fires are various kinds of seamless goo, like spray-on foam, fire-taped gypsum sheathing, or the most featureless of all surfaces, that ubiquitous material called "Drivit." These seamless goos themselves have none of what an architect would call tectonic integrity, and the Building Inspector insists that they be slathered over every material and every juncture of materials that might have that quality.

The Value Engineer is in charge of making things as cheaply as possible, and he is given special powers when it comes to housing, for the good and simple reason that most people can't afford most housing. He hates with passion all that good, solid stuff that tectonic integrity is based upon.

An architect called before the Grand Inquisitors is in a terrible fix. His own belief system is so deeply rooted that it is unshakeable, but he finds himself forced to believe something contradictory at the same time. Freud called this kind of situation *ein verdoppeltes Verbindung* (a double bind), and he thought it was the cause of schizophrenia. Some architects do, in fact, go mad. Others simply renounce their beliefs, enter the bordello, and are reborn as *marketects,* purveyors of stylistic kitsch made of synthetic materials. Some marketects do this willingly, and some find pleasure in it, but others retain enough of their original belief system to be wracked by lifelong guilt.

For various reasons, the Grand Inquisitors do not have jurisdiction everywhere. In England, for instance, the Tribunal has less of a strangle-hold than in the United States. In the United States, expensive buildings for wealthy institutions are outside the Inquisitors' reach, as are detached houses out in the country. Lots of architects begin their careers doing country houses in the hope of one day designing expensive buildings for wealthy institutions, thereby avoiding the Tribunal altogether. Or they can teach. None of the Grand Inquisitors has ever set foot in a school of architecture, and teachers and students have never heard of the Tribunal.

All of this would be a reasonable and sustainable arrangement, ex-cept for two things. First is what happens to the city. With the Tribunal firmly in charge of all the normal building in the city, it gets uglier and crummier all the time. Second is what happens to architects. There are only so many expensive institutional buildings, fancy houses, and tenure-track teaching jobs. Architects are like a fecund species with a diminished habitat and inadequate fodder. They turn on their own kind and become vicious, cannibalistic, and weird.

These knotty questions surrounding the issues of style, truth, and technology have preoccupied many people. The two best-known and most-publicized attempts within the New Urbanist camp to provide an-swers to them are those in Seaside, Florida, and the Disney new town, Cel-ebration, also in Florida. In very different ways, each of these places puts forth a proposition that is profoundly unsatisfactory for the normal task of building city fabric.

Seaside is a small town of notably well made buildings that are substantial, solid, and "real" feeling in a way that is not captured in pho-tographs. No vinyl siding here. In part because of these qualities, it is ac-tually a much more congenial place to be than one would imagine from all the mountains of press coverage, the books about it, or the devastat-ing burlesque of it in the film *The Truman Show.* Andres Duany and Eliz-abeth Plater-Zyberg, the planners of Seaside, set in motion the mecha-nism that has produced this solid result, with an elegant prescription in the Seaside Design Code. It says simply, "No building material shall simulate another material." This idea, straight from the heart of the Arts and Crafts movement, became one of the fundamental ideas of modern architecture. It is also an ideal rarely attained in normal contemporary building practice. Its realization at Seaside helps make an admirable place, but, like the best products of the Arts and Crafts, one that is rarefied and only replicable in equally rarefied circumstances. Seaside's qualities could not have been achieved without the fanatical devotion and impeccable taste of Robert and Darryl Davis, its developers, or their painstakingly assembled corps of elite builders. Seaside is a fine achievement, but not a model in all respects.

Celebration has two problems of a very different sort. Its design code, written by New Urbanist Ray Gindroz, prescribes a series of historic building styles, just like the marketing folk want. The code is intended to lift this sort of operation out of the realm of kitsch by showing builders how to get the historic styles right—*marchitecture* with real scholarship. An obvious problem is the cultural ossification implied in such a prescription, the total denial of the architect's inexorably implanted vision of himself as the appointed messenger of the future and the scientist operating from first principles. The legacy of Gropius et al. is far too deeply embedded to be dislodged by something like the Celebration Design Code.

The other problem is more serious. The Celebration code may appease one of the three Grand Inquisitors, the Marketing Director, but it has nothing whatever to say to the other two, the Code Enforcer and the Value Engineer. Historic styles made in synthetic materials by lousy, uncaring workers may look all right in photographs, but close at hand the experience is like snuggling up to a face-lift and silicone implants—shocking and creepy for those reared on the ideal of tectonic truth.

There is, however, a kind of architecture based on an alternative form of truth that avoids all of these problems. It is based on a subject the Tribunal has no rules about and doesn't care about, and it satisfies an architect's inner need to be a messenger of truth and not just a purveyor of kitsch. At least it satisfies mine, and I think it does the same for others. The subject is urbanism, the history of the city. Truth about the city is not the only kind of truth upon which an architect can ground his lifework, but it is a good kind of truth for at least three reasons:

1. It is good because it is comprehensible and meaningful to large numbers of people. There is nothing hermetic or esoteric about it.

2. It is good because it does not have the forces of the Inquisition directed against it.

3. It is good because it allows architects to engage in "healthy intercourse with the city" (Colin Rowe's memorable phrase) without entering the bordello.

Urbanism as the underpinning of an architectural aesthetic is sensible, because it allows architects to spend their days in noble combat with one (not all) of the forms of diminished experience inflicted by the monster who grew to his fierce maturity between 1945 and 1965 and has been raging through the world ever since. Two sets of ideas about building are leading the architectural world out of the miasma of stylistic fratricide, theoretical hermeticism, conceptual masturbation, and other forms of self-inflicted irrelevance in which it has been stuck for so long. These two sets of ideas can be loosely labeled *urbanism* and *environmentalism*. Bundling these two broad movements together is a fundamentally difficult proposition, but to some degree and under certain circumstances, urbanism and environmentalism can be made congruent, mutually reinforcing, and powerful.

PART 4

URBANISM

Parts 1 to 3 have presented the basis for a kind of action that is gratifying and meaningful to those engaged in it. That activity is urbanism, the making and remaking of parts of cities. The Grand Inquisitors make it impossible to do certain kinds of admirable architecture in many normal circumstances, but the Inquisitors can't really stop us from the practice of urbanism. It is a gratifying activity because it allows its practitioners forms of engagement in the world that combine the grand strategic thinking of Alice Waters with the earthy pragmatism of Julia Child. Like both of those great ladies of the kitchen, urbanists deal with the quality of daily life and the assaults made upon it in the name of progress and modernity in the middle of the twentieth century. At this point, the counterreformation of food culture is much further along than the counterreformation of urban culture, and canned string beans are more anachronistic than suburban business parks, with their faceless buildings swimming in an ocean of parking. Canned string beans appear to have been out of production for some time, but the ocean of parking is still growing.

The activity of urbanism lifts the proscriptions on experiences that became forbidden fruit when we took our vows and donned the cassock of modernity. We, almost all of us at once, came to believe that the intimacy of Bologna, the grandeur of Paris, the civility of Charleston, and the throbbing life of Shanghai were like the pleasures of a museum—things we could look at but never own, let alone make for ourselves. We all knew that, while it might be worthwhile for some bookish types to become con-servators and curators of these sorts of things, the pleasures of these cit-ies were not the stuff of our times. They came from *other times,* before modernity, before our ordination as messengers of the new.

To some orders of monks, the joys of conversation, the flesh, or the palate are forbidden. The joy of music was forbidden to the Taliban. Colin Rowe laid bare the screwball dialectics that forbade the pleasures of the street, the courtyard, and the market square to us. Partially it was the on-slaught of our technologies that made urbanity seem so exotic and re-mote. But more than technologies themselves, it was what we believed about technology that launched us into an era in which we systematically unlearned basic things, known throughout the world for millennia, about the making of our habitat. We attributed to the imperatives of new tech-nologies the idea that buildings should be independent, idealized things, not parts of places, giving shape to the town around them.

An attractive aspect of the practice of urbanism is that it can take place in an imperfect world. No one seriously thinks of a contemporary city as a potential *Gesamtkunstwerk*, flawless in every detail, like the house in which the architect designs the ashtrays and places all the fur-niture. An architect, or anyone else involved in city building, does not feel the need to reform everything about everything in order to improve something about something. One does not need to repeal the automobile or the manufacture of sheetrock to build a lovely courtyard. A couple of decades ago, the course of the world seemed intractable, as if there were nothing one could do about it. Humanity seemed doomed to habitat a world that was ever more synthetic, more placeless, more polluted, and less endearing. Urbanism, as it is now practiced by people in many related disciplines, shows otherwise.

The essays of Part 4 revolve around episodes from the practice of urbanism and attempt to convey at least one version of its content.

At Home

Spending most of a lifetime in a nice little city like San Francisco is especially good training for an urbanist. Other small, urbane cities, such as Lausanne, or Strasbourg, or American ones like Philadelphia or Seattle, teach the same lessons. If all architects and town planners were forced to have such an experience before they built anything, the world would look different and probably much better.

San Francisco is based upon a mid-nineteenth-century town plan that has remained remarkably intact through the most tumultuous changes in transportation technology, demographics, planning ideas, and the underlying economy of the place. It was a frontier village that suddenly became an international port commanding a vast hinterland, then later a transcontinental railhead and manufacturing center. It was for a long time the center of banking and finance in the West and was the main port of embarkation for the Pacific in World War II. In the last half of the twentieth century, the port died, manufacturing left, the railroads disappeared, much of the city's banking and finance dispersed to other places, and there was a determined, well-financed attempt by an entire generation to reshape the heart of the city through urban renewal and federal highway programs. Recently, the city went through a drastic convulsion caused by the boom and bust of the Internet economy.

As the city lived through these changes, it also generated a sprawling city-region that became a new kind of economic force, one recognized long ago by Jane Jacobs in *The Economy of Cities* (and more recently by Peter Calthorpe in *The Regional City*) as the fundamental unit of a new global economy. In the midst of this, the city was reborn, not in the new form envisaged by postwar planners, but in a way much more closely related to the original city of the mid–nineteenth century. The largest Canadian and American development organizations have made repeated attempts to capitalize on the resiliency and success of the city, and while their impact is not negligible, their successes are far overshadowed by legions of small builders and investors. It is not the same city with the same economy, culture, or technologies as the nineteenth-century city, but the physical structure that sustains vigorous life in the early twenty-first century is rooted in principles that have outlived multiple attempts to supplant them. While political processes and economic forces continually reshape San Francisco, there is an unseen hand at work, through which patterns of blocks, streets, and buildings that were established long ago reassert themselves.

An architect confronting this phenomenon every day learns two things. First, he learns to build in relation to this unseen structure of the city, a structure that is bigger, older, more important, and more deeply loved than anything he and his clients can conceive on their own. Second, he learns how these kinds of urban structures are created, what they consist of, and the huge difference between their presence and their absence. Much of the city-region around San Francisco was built from scratch in the last fifty years, without the benefit of the kind of urban history that sustains the city itself. The contrast is so sharp that the architect acquires at least the aspiration to give structure to structureless places, and bit by bit learns how to go about it.

Most of our work as architects and as urban designers in San Francisco falls within the maps that define the original nineteenth-century block structure and lot platting that give the city its character. All of the buildings we have designed are made by normative and inexpensive means—that is, they are within the jurisdiction of the three Grand Inquisitors and needed unanimous approval from the Tribunal to be built. This work began more than twenty-five years ago and continues today in the two very different arenas of individual buildings and large-scale urban planning. Urban planning and architecture are, or can be, two parts of the enterprise of urbanism. Whatever meaning or value our architecture may have comes not from tectonic qualities that are unattainable in normal cheap building practice but from its qualities as a constituent part of the city.

The operative principle at both scales is urban repair as opposed to urban renewal, but it does not consist simply of putting back the nineteenth-century city just as it was. This is for two reasons: first, because the world is profoundly different from the way it was in 1870, and second, because it definitely *is* possible to improve upon the city as it was. Berlin's great urbanist Joseph Paul Kleiheuss coined the term "critical reconstruction" in relation to the 1980s interventions that he directed, and his successor Hans Stimmann has carried forward that idea in all of his work. I like to think that our San Francisco work is "critical reconstruction" of a similar spirit. Its intention is to establish a living connection between the *genius loci* of the city, its physical structure and history, and whatever new and novel circumstances befall it.

This critical reconstruction has just a few very simple strategies. First is the reconstruction of street walls, surfaces of buildings of sufficient continuity and consistency that they define the space of streets. This is hardly a new idea, but the role of normal building fabric as the shaper of the public realm of streets is axiomatic for any urban place, not just San Francisco. For seventy years or so, modernists and their children and grandchildren have been claiming that there can be urbanity without streets or urban streets whose edges are not defined by buildings. Even Mumford looked forward to "the houseless street and the streetless house." But despite the billions upon billions of dollars and every other currency that has been invested in their ideas, there is not a single satisfactory urban place in the world that does not follow the universal axiom that buildings must define the space of streets. Cities where handsome, life-sustaining urban fabric is made from modern architecture—Vancouver, Miami Beach, Tel Aviv, now parts of Berlin—do so by rejecting the modernist canon of the freestanding building and reestablishing the traditional idea of the street wall. Time has proved beyond a doubt that Le Corbusier, Giedion, and their crowd were simply wrong on this subject.

This does not mean that *all* buildings must define streets, because monuments and some civic buildings are important and necessary exceptions. Frank Gehry's tour de force at Bilboa, framed by the fabric of the historic city, is just fine, as is Santiago Calatrava's spectacular Milwaukee Museum of Art, jutting out into Lake Michigan. The great message of Colin Rowe's black plans is that such buildings are exceptions— the normative buildings that constitute the fabric of the city *must* define streets; there is simply no other way to make a city. This reverses the modernist dogma of the liberated, self-referential building, and this is one of the very few places in the subtle, complicated discussion of urbanism that a little simpleminded dogmatism is exactly what is called for.

The second principle is a more ambiguous one that has to do with parcelization, the size of lots and how land is owned. Probably the earliest European urbanist to react to the grossness of postwar reconstruction was Aldo Rossi's teacher at the University of Rome, Saverio Muratori. For Muratori, the history of the city was the history of *property*, and his favored tool of urban analysis was the parcel map. Anne Vernez Moudon's seminal book on San Francisco, *Built for Change*, includes Muratori-like maps of the original blocks and lots. Much of our work in San Francisco has been a reconstruction or a partial reconstruction of the parcelization shown on her maps, because it is that enduring structure of small lots that is so fundamental to the scale and character of the city. Much of our work was done, however, after the urban renewal planners of the 1950s and 1960s had systematically erased not only lot lines but many blocks and streets as well. Putting back eradicated nineteenth-century lot lines through the agency of bureaucracies and development organizations larger than those of the nineteenth century is not a simple matter, nor is it something one can make rigid rules about. Sometimes the massing and articulation of buildings can relate buildings on large parcels to the architecture of small parcels, but such an operation clumsily done can also produce the most dreadful kitsch. After experiments with mandating this sort of thing, I have arrived at the reluctant conclusion that it is usually a matter better left to the skill of architects than incorporated into the prescriptions of planning codes.

The third principle has to do with life in the middle of blocks. Relentless gridiron cities can be dismal, boring places, but San Francisco is not. One reason for this is the way that generation after generation of small interventions has created richness and complexity within the blocks of the grid. Part of this richness comes from what people have made of midblock lanes that were platted in the original surveyor's maps of some sectors of the city. San Francisco has hundreds of beautiful little alleys where people sink roots and carefully make their homes. Also, usually hidden from streets are networks of courtyards tucked away in the middle of blocks. Courtyards are places where cats live, where vegetables grow, where conversation occurs, where in some places laundry still hangs, and where urban densities are made not only tolerable but nurturing.

The ever-changing limitations of craft and material make the reproduction of historic *architecture* a doomed proposition. As with most cosmetic surgery, the artifice is transparent, unconvincing, and sad. Even Las Vegas's most lavish and expensive simulations are not expected by their creators to be mistaken for anything real. But historic *urbanism* is another matter. It is possible and perfectly legitimate to build courts and alleys that function in precisely the same way as those of the nineteenth century. Just like the old ones, these new courts and alleys can be authentic receptacles for real life. Unlike the houses of Disney's Celebration, they are not diminished or falsified by their rendering in the materials and craft approved by the terrible Tribunal.

Again, the lesson of the black plans is that urbanism is a *spatial* matter; fancy materials are not crucial. Some great cities, such as Chicago, have special qualities because they are so solidly built, but other great cities, such as St. Petersburg, are made of bubble gum. Peter the Great spent most of his rubles on drainage, hydrology, and canals, and the buildings themselves are made like stage sets. San Francisco is closer to St. Petersburg than to Chicago in this regard.

The "critical" part of critical reconstruction is looking at the historic city and seeing its deficiencies or noting where similar circumstances are addressed differently, perhaps better in other cities or in other ways. One significant aspect of the historic block patterns of San Francisco is *not* so good, not nearly so good as in the residential fabrics of similar scale and density in Milan, Bologna, Berlin, and Beijing, to name a few. All of those cities also have good streets and interesting midblocks, but each has in abundance what San Francisco typically lacks: networks of passages that connect streets to the middles of blocks and make midblocks visible from streets.

The historic center of Bologna is so beautiful it can bring you to tears. What make it that way are the passages from streets through buildings to courtyards and from courtyard to courtyard. Anyone can walk through some of the courts, but some are private and gated. The art of the gate itself, the transparent metal membrane that separates the places anyone can go from those that belong to just a few people, is an essential part of the urbanism of Bologna.

Some Berliners clearly understood the lessons of medieval Bologna at the beginning of the twentieth century, and the newly restored blocks of the 1905 Hackischer Hof are a glory of city building, very much like the *centro storico* of Bologna. Seven beautiful courtyards are linked to streets and to one another through a series of narrow passages, usually two or three stories high, penetrating the six-story housing blocks. The fact that, as soon as its restoration was completed, Hackisher Hof immediately became a stylish, expensive address, with shops and restaurants hidden back in the courtyards doing a booming business, suggests that the lessons of urbanism don't go out of style. The construction techniques and architectural stylistics of Hackischer Hof are unremarkable examples of *fin de siècle* vernacular—and that is precisely the point. Hackisher Hof is made of normative, inexpensive construction and is a great and enduring place because of its qualities as urban space and nothing else. Urbanism is enough.

Our critical reconstructions of San Francisco lots and blocks are attempts to apply all of these observations. They restore street walls, they restore the life of midblocks, and they create passages between streets and midblocks that are not part of an inherited local legacy but are a lesson learned from other places. This application of the *passagio Bolognese* to San Francisco blocks has also been used to address urban conditions that did not exist when the city's original plat maps were drawn. Part of San Francisco's struggle in the last half century has been to remain a viable pedestrian city as it has become increasingly a part of a regional economy in a totally auto-dominated region. San Franciscans do things all over the Bay Area, and they have to drive to get where they need to go. Parking large numbers of cars in a way that does not destroy streetscapes and does not generate the prohibitive costs of underground garages is a big problem. In many cases, the passage from street to midblock has provided the answer. One narrow passage can serve as the driveway for a dozen cars or more, and they can be dispersed in small garages that cost a fraction of a large concrete parking podium. The few cars that use a passage move slowly, and they can be mixed with pedestrians as in a European *woonerf*. Cars are present and accessible as discreet instruments of service, not as the dominant feature of the townscape.

Passages from streets to midblocks also help to address another problem of the modern city that San Francisco's nineteenth-century builders never thought about. American cities are in direct competition with their own suburbs. The pathologies of urban violence and crime have fueled suburbanization and the abandonment of central cities, and San Francisco housing must be, and appear to be, as safe as its suburban competition. Passages provide a means of making gated places and securing courtyards and routes through projects without turning streetscapes into bastions of paranoid insularity. Danger in cities is nothing new, and one can learn from the grace with which ancient places separated public from private and used passages to allow the glimpse of a private court to enrich the public street.

These basic strategies of critical reconstruction are what I have had the good fortune to learn from a place that people defended against the onslaught of postwar planning but which went through fundamental political and economic transformations nonetheless. I live in a city that has changed and remained the same simultaneously. As technological transformations and the force of globalization persist, as they surely will, this process of changing while staying the same becomes crucial throughout the world.

The Twelfth Map

The normal working day of a town planner has a very different flavor from that of an architect. As one who does both, the difference is clear to me. When an architect is designing a building that is likely to be built, there is never the slightest doubt that what he is doing will have an affect on somebody's life. Most architects, when they find themselves in flights of self-absorbed self-indulgence, have the decency to feel at least a twinge of guilt. In most situations, town planning doesn't work quite the same way. The likelihood that what one proposes will ever actually occur, or will occur soon enough that one would have to deal with real human consequences, seems so very remote. Town planning, as one is in the midst of it, feels more like writing fiction or playing chess—infinitely absorbing, but not all that consequential in a direct and immediate way. Town planners would feel differently about their trade, however, if they were to study the historical maps of places like San Francisco. If you thoroughly deconstructed the decisions, thought process, and politics that produced the good parts and the not-so-good parts of San Francisco, you would never again think of town planning as an abstract activity like chess. San Francisco's maps and the stories they tell are filled with lessons for other places.

The least attractive and most congested part of San Francisco is right in the center of town, just south of the intersection where the city's two biggest streets, Van Ness Avenue and the great diagonal of Market Street, cross obliquely. In this area of a dozen blocks or so, the clarity and grace of the rest of the City give way to total confusion. Very large streets run every which way and meet five or six to an intersection. The shortest routes to the major regional highways and the Bay Bridge run through here, but they are so indirect and confusing that even cab drivers will frequently take a long way round in order not to drive here. The cut-up land begets numerous, large, misshapen buildings that are among the ugliest in town. It is such a disorienting place that most lifetime residents of the city cannot draw a half-correct map of it from memory. Though it could not be more centrally located or better served by regional highways, it has always been marginal real estate, even when the city is booming. It is a miserable place to drive, worse to walk, and lethal on a bicycle.

The impetus for studying this area of the city comes indirectly from the Loma Prieta earthquake of 1989, which severely damaged the Central Freeway, which passed directly over this area south of Market Street and then rammed brutally through the once-fine Hayes Valley Neighborhood to the north. Incredibly, the elevated Central Freeway was routed directly in front of the great domed structure of Arthur Brown's magnificent City Hall. As a great civic building, Les Invalides in Paris has nothing on San Francisco City Hall, but the highway planners of the 1950s thought it was perfectly OK to run a double-deck elevated freeway right past its front door.

The freeway was so universally hated in the city that the electorate would not stand for the State's plans to repair it after the earthquake. During the first *eleven years* that city and state officials diddled with the fate of this prime real estate, former city planning director Alan Jacobs and a group of citizens took it upon themselves to devise an alternative to the freeway reconstruction. The result was a beautiful design for a boulevard to replace the freeway north of Market Street. The boulevard was pitted against the State's freeway replacement design in a citywide referendum and won convincingly, but the boulevard design, fine as it is, leaves many problems unaddressed. There is still a great scar where the freeway was removed near City Hall and northward. And there is an unresolved mess of tangled streets and fragmented land south of Market Street where a new shortened freeway segment will be brought down at the most awkward place possible to join surface streets. The Hayes Valley Neighborhood, now spontaneously regenerating itself in the wake of the freeway removal, is cut through by citywide traffic routed in every direction through the grid in complicated Z-shaped routes. In some places, pairs of one-way streets, each carrying lots of traffic, actually meet head-on.

In the thirteen years since the Loma Prieta earthquake, we have tried several times to help the City repair these unresolved conditions and the wound inflicted by the Central Freeway. In the course of these unfulfilled efforts, we have learned some interesting things about an intractable puzzle that has been made worse by successive attempts to make it better for the last hundred years or so. As we have come to understand this story with all its twists and turns, we have seen that it is not just about this particular place; it is about the genealogy of many American neighborhoods and cities. To make this genealogy clear, we have redrawn the maps that mark the major milestones of the story in the same manner and at the same scale.

Our redrawn version of the original 1849 Jasper O'Farrell survey of the area shows that the structure of the neighborhood and the roots of its later problems were established with the first hasty marks made on the virgin land. The map shows that, from the very outset, this area was the confluence of three different grids of streets, each with different dimensions and orientations. On the bottom of the map is a little grid of streets, the orientation of which was established by the eighteenth-century Spanish Mission Do-

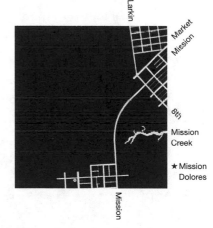

Three grids; the O'Farrell map, 1849

lores to the south and the Mission Plank Road, extending from the Mission northward. The plank road bends around to the east and joins a grid of large blocks oriented with Market Street, the main boulevard of the new settlement. Market Street is oriented diagonally to the principal grid of the city, a much finer grained grid of streets and blocks that has from the very beginning supported city fabric of a particularly attractive and livable scale. The streets of the north of Market grid strike Market Street in an irregular pattern with no continuity to the south of Market grid.

Resolving the grids; the Eddy map, 1851

The 1851 map, drawn by surveyor William Eddy, shows the beginning of his long struggle to resolve the problems created by O'Farrell's original platting. Eddy used the radius of the plank road to generate a great hemicycle joining the east/west streets of the south of Market grid to the Mission grid, and he resolved the collision of geometries with an elegantly shaped little park, now partially occupied by an awkward building that houses the San Francisco Department of City Planning and a rent-a-car lot. In a neat example of how the stuff of life fills the vessel of the city, the last one hundred square feet or so of the triangular tip of the rent-a-car lot, the part of Eddy's elegant park that is too small to fit a car into, is now occupied by a crepe-making pushcart with four outdoor tables doing a robust business. The clever resolutions of the 1851 map still do not address the difficult north/south connections across Market Street.

The map of 1870 shows the final result of the work of Eddy and his generation. The north of Market grid has been extended westward as the Western Addition. The fabric of the Western Addition is interrupted by four major public spaces: Lafayette Square, Alamo Square, Duboce Park, and the new Civic Center, which contains City Hall. City Hall is sited at the termination of both Fulton Street, north of Market, and a northward extension of Eighth Street across Market Street, another inspired answer to a problem created in the original map. This siting of City Hall achieves the difficult linkage of the two differently oriented grids across the diagonal of Market Street and provides a monumental setting at the termination of two major streets. Adjustments have also been made at the intersections of Ninth and

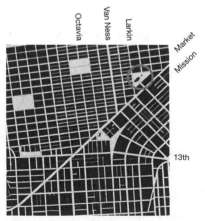

The Western Addition, 1870
(City Hall circled)

Tenth and Market to provide reasonable connections of the grids north and south. Most of the blocks of the Western Addition and many of those south of Market have been bisected by small lanes, which to this day provide San Francisco with some of its most charming and humane settings for city life. All of this work represents nineteenth-century American urbanism at its very finest. It consists of a complex series of subtle adjustments that elegantly resolve the problems created when grids were hastily drawn to organize land speculation under the pressure of settlement during the Gold Rush.

In 1905, the great man from Chicago Daniel Burnham produced a visionary proposal for a twentieth-century transformation of San Francisco. He thought that what this lovely nineteenth-century city really needed was a big dose of the grandeur of the Farnese Popes and Napoleon III. At a colossal scale, he superimposed literal quotes from Baroque Rome and Hausmann's Paris onto the map of San Francisco, like an urban design student who has just learned to use a scanner. Huge expropriations, like the urban renewal proposals of a

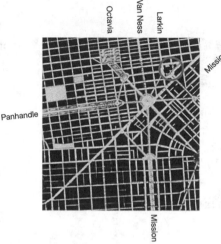

The Burnham plan, 1905 (City Hall circled)

later generation, cut through the fabric of the city with great diagonals, shattering Eddy's elegant reconciliation's of the original grids. The intersection of Market and Van Ness became the Piazza dei Popolo, with the famous trivium of via di Ripetta, via del Corso, and via Babuino represented by (1) a new boulevard extending all the way across town from Golden Gate Park to the west, (2) a much grander version of the old Eleventh Street, and (3) a prescient vision of a new connection forced south from Van Ness to Mission Street. He did recognize the brilliance of Eddy's siting of the City Hall at the north end of Eighth Street, and he proposed a grandiose new baroque edifice at the same location. There is also a huge curving boulevard that swings through south of Market and then cuts through the north of Market grid, anticipating the alignment of the Central Freeway in 1957. Like many of his contemporaries, Burnham had a foot in the nineteenth century and a foot in the twentieth. His nineteenth-century foot was his neo-classical formalism; his twentieth-century or modernist foot was his grandiosity and hubris. Burnham was deadly serious about his bombastic plan, and at the height of his career in 1905, he took the train from Chicago to San Francisco to spend two weeks supervising its printing. There is no reason to think that Burnham's versions of expropriation and planning by demolition would have left the City any less fragmented and screwed up than what actually happened much later.

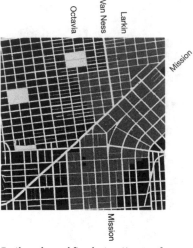

Earthquake and fire destruction, 1906

Just a few months after the publication of Burnham's plan came the earthquake and fire of 1906, which completely destroyed most of the city, including the large area shown in grey on the adjacent map. It is significant that the leaders and citizens of San Francisco completely rejected Burnham's proposals when they had the opportunity to implement them. Burnham's sponsors, the "progressive" ex-mayor John Phelan and his cohorts, lost their struggle with the incumbent and massively corrupt mayor Sunny Jim Bradley. With only one major revision, the nineteenth-century city was faithfully reconstructed and remained intact almost until World War II. Because the Victorian fabric that had been constructed over many decades was rebuilt in its original form all at once, San Francisco acquired the largest, latest, and most consistent fabric of Victorian architecture anywhere in the world—six years after the death of Queen Victoria. By then, Sunny Jim Bradley's vision was practically a revival movement. To Burnham, his protégé, the protomodern architect Willis Polk, and their sponsor Phelan, Sunny Jim's reconstruction of San Francisco was a tragic lost opportunity.

The one major revision of the city after the earthquake was the City Beautiful plan of the Civic Center by Arthur Brown and John Bakewell, executed in the 1920s. The Civic Center is a grand place with many fine qualities, but it does sever the ingenious connection to the south of Market grid that Eddy had achieved and that Burnham proposed to reinforce. What Burnham et al. called a "lost opportunity" is an early twentieth-century reconstruction of a slightly modified nineteenth-century town plan. It is, in fact, the city that people today admire and love, the city that is a convention and tourist mecca. It was the setting for the Dashiell Hammett mysteries, the great atmospheric movies made from them, and scores of films and TV shows ever since. It is the city that, despite massive political and administrative problems, year in and year out sustains the most hyper-inflated real estate market in North America.

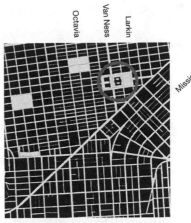

The city rebuilds, 1906–1930 (Civic Center circled)

In 1931, the era of the automobile began in earnest in San Francisco, even before the Works Progress Administration built the city's two great bridges, the Golden Gate and the Bay Bridge, linking the city to its suburbs north and east. An earlier and less spectacular connection was made to the south as Highway 101 was brought up Potrero Boulevard and linked to Van Ness Avenue, leading to the Golden Gate Bridge by a large new street called South Van Ness. This new street tore through the most ingenious part of Eddy's map on exactly the same alignment as the western leg of Burnham's trivium. As the

The auto era begins, 1931 (South Van Ness circled)

city began its modern role as the center of a sprawling city-region and faced its first confrontation with regional automobile infrastructure, its nineteenth-century fabric began to come unraveled. The 1931 map shows the devastating effect of South Van Ness. All of the blocks it cuts through are left as tattered, odd-shaped remnants, and each of its intersections are impossible confrontations of multiple streets from every angle.

After World War II, there were two types of large plans for the area, each as filled with hubris and grandiosity as Burnham's, each as contemptuous of the existing city. Amazingly, these two kinds of planning, which were both carried forward with the momentum of federal funding, had nothing whatever to do with each other and were the products of totally separate bureaucracies. As became common in the years after the war, the planning of roads and the planning of neighborhoods were separate activities conducted by specialists, each of whom knew little and cared less about the other. The separation of buildings and roads preached by Le Corbusier and Gideon became an unbreachable separation of decision making and funding that persists almost unchallenged to this day.

Urban renewal as proposed, 1950–1965

The proposals for urban renewal and those for new highways are shown here as separate maps. The urban renewal map is a composite of various plans put forward by the redevelopment authorities in San Francisco between 1948 and 1965, including the Mel Scott/T. J. Kent *New City*. All of the urban renewal ideas were similar. Like the *New City*, they systematically erased the nineteenth-century map, with its delicate scale of small blocks subdivided by lanes and individual lots. Parcel lines and lanes disappear altogether, and blocks are merged. The *New City* plan combined thirty blocks, each with at least one midblock lane, into seven undivided superblocks.

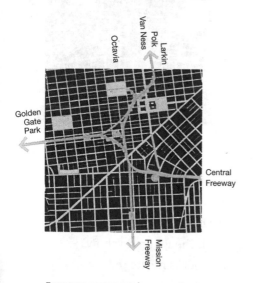

Freeways as proposed, 1950–1965

The highway plans were even more radical, with double-deck elevated highways tearing through the South of Market neighborhood and Hayes Valley, then branching in two directions and heading all through the city, through major parks and along the waterfront. The planning and construction of the highways began in the early fifties and continued until what is known in local oral histories as "the Freeway Revolt" in 1965.

There were some amazing characters associated with this revolution, one of whom happened to be San Francisco's flamboyant and combative former mayor Joseph Alioto. The one and only time I ever spoke to Joe Alioto was around 1996, shortly before his death, and thirty years or so after his last mayoral term. Two nights before, I had seen an astonishing film clip on PBS of Joe Alioto's finest hour—his 1965 testimony to the Senate Highway Appropriations subcommittee. Fifteen or so of the largest figures in the Senate were assaulting him in the most intimidating fashion possible for San Francisco's refusal to accept federal highway funds or to permit the completion of the city's network of elevated freeways that had been planned for fifteen years. If the Congress for the New Urbanism gave out its own Congressional Medals of Honor, it should bestow a posthumous one on Joe Alioto for his solo performance that day. He told the senators (on TV) that he knew who financed their campaigns, and he went into some compelling detail about the relationships of these senators to General Motors, U.S. Steel, and the other big players in the highway lobby. He said that there was no way that he or the citizens of San Francisco would let this self-serving consortium of special interest wreck their treasure of a city, as it clearly intended to do. He told them that day that their game was over, and in one important sense, it was. The great octopus of elevated highways that was scheduled to run all through San Francisco's most delicate neighborhoods, through the panhandle of Golden Gate Park and all along the city's most scenic stretches of bay shore, never grew another inch. It was a pivotal moment for many American cities, not just San Francisco. For the first time, local officials saw that they could say no to the federal highway juggernaut that was tearing through inner-city neighborhoods all over the country.

The day that I went up to Joe Alioto and congratulated him, three decades after the fact, for what he said and did in 1965, we were standing in the sunshine, both carrying baskets loaded with beautiful organic produce from the Ferry Plaza Farmer's Market, organized by Sibella Kraus and others, right where the Embarcadero Freeway had cast its shadow for almost thirty-five years. In his late eighties at the time, Alioto was still a politician to the bone. I had never been within a hundred feet of him before, but he put down his basket and took my free hand in both of his and said, "Dan, it is *so* good to see you again."

Joe Alioto and the Freeway Fighters of the 1960s stopped the expansion of the freeway network, but they did not repair the damage done to the city between 1950 and 1965. Despite the efforts of virtually everyone in the planning professions in San Francisco, most of the neighborhood groups, a lot of traffic and transportation people, and a succession of mayors starting with Alioto and including Diane Feinstein, the freeway network as it was built in 1965 would be intact today, except for one small segment, had Northern California's most effective regional planning agency, the San Andreas Fault, not intervened with the Loma Prieta earthquake of 1989.

In the 1960s, for a whole series of reasons, the dreams of the postwar generation lost their authority, but no new, enlightened process of decision making has ever taken their place. In 1971, an outraged citizen leaped over the dais at a public hearing, seized San Francisco's all-powerful redevelopment czar, Justin Herman, by the neck, and choked him. He died shortly afterward. The new activism of the 1960s and early 1970s stopped the construction of urban highways and the vast clearance projects of urban renewal with a ferocious mode of discourse employed to this day by all sides of all questions in San Francisco. Tom Wolfe's classic sketch *Mau-Mauing the Flak Catchers* memorializes the way conversations about planning take place in San Francisco, a process that has produced much more paralysis than action.

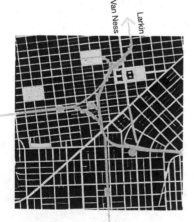

Urban renewal and freeways as implemented, 1950–1965

Radical activism stopped the postwar planners, but not until the face of San Francisco, like most American cities, had been altered substantially. The map below shows the combined effects of urban renewal and freeway construction as they were executed. North of Market, the delicate scale of the original grid is in stark contrast to the gross superblocks that the planners of urban renewal thought would make better places. This complicated hybrid is the condition that San Franciscans have lived with and grown used to for more than thirty-five years—partially the early-twentieth-century reconstruction of a

nineteenth century town plan, partially
the half-realized vision of postwar planners and highway bureaucrats intent on
eradicating the old plan.

In the fourteen years since Loma
Prieta the map has improved in one
significant way. The most egregious part
of the Central Freeway, the part right in
front of City Hall, was badly damaged
and removed, not repaired. This spurred a
spontaneous revival of a portion of Hayes
Valley, but the district as a whole has remained in its unresolved state of limbo.

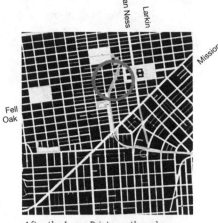

After the Loma Prieta earthquake
(Removed freeway section circled.)

The way out of this unsatisfactory hybrid is not easy, mostly because the
politics of San Francisco are so extraordinarily fractious. However, in the
decades that populist militancy has been standard operating procedure in
San Francisco planning, there has probably never been a situation like this
one, in which everyone, or virtually everyone among the citizenry, agrees.
What is valued and loved about the center of San Francisco by the most
wildly diverse citizens is the residue of the nineteenth century city plan.
What is universally despised is what planners did to the city from the late
1930s onward. You can be dressed in a basic black sheath with pearls or in
combat fatigues with a femur through your nose, and your opinions on
this matter are likely to be the same.

Consensus among citizens in a public process, and consensus
among the city's politicians and among and within rival bureaucracies,
are different things, however. Diplomatic relations between the Bloods
and the Crips of South Central Los Angeles are more constructive and
cordial than those among contending politicians and their surrogates in
San Francisco. Though I have never agreed with Burnham's proposals for
San Francisco, it is easy to sympathize with his exasperation. Many things
contribute to the situation in which no one can implement a major structural change in the city. Partially it is the old modernist separation of
buildings from roads that bred separate bureaucracies for each; partially
it is populist mistrust of top-down decision making after the brutal mis-

takes of Urban Renewal; partially it is class warfare over turf in a successful real estate market. It all adds up to a paralysis in which the collection of tools that has come together in the new Urbanist tool kit—Cornell figure/ground drawings, Muratori-style parcel maps, block plans and building typologies, the "critical reconstruction" methods of Kleiheuse and Stimmann—cannot be fully unleashed on the problems of the city.

Though it seems inconceivable that a bold physical plan could make it through the political minefield of San Francisco, it is not hard to conceive the physical dimensions of such a plan. Most of what could and should be done is so obvious that it takes no special knowledge to see. All of the seven-plus acres of land freed by the tearing down of the freeway north of Market Street, including the slivers along the new Octavia Boulevard, should be rebuilt as town fabric, as housing and neighborhood-serving businesses. The mid-rise height limits adjacent to the former freeway right-of-way should be adjusted downward to match the Hayes Valley Neighborhood around them. On three of the former freeway sites, there are opportunities to create new midblock lanes, connecting to historic ones and reinforcing the legacy of Eddy's plan. In 1992 we built one such lane, and it has been a place so well regarded by both neighbors and residents that taking advantage of the opportunity to make more such places seems an obvious strategy.

Less obvious is what should be done south of Market, because what is clearly the right solution is politically impossible for the immediate future. That would be to tear down another half dozen blocks of the freeway and bring it down to grade at the point where the city grid could most easily absorb and disperse its impact of regional traffic and allow the entire Eddy resolution of the south of Market grids to be restored. That solution would include an extension of the new Alan Jacobs–designed Octavia Boulevard south to the new freeway touchdown. Of all the alternatives that have been considered, this one would be far and away the best for the needs of regional traffic, for the creation of development opportunities, including new housing, and for the physical grace of the city. The difficult legislative compromise that was reached between the City and the state highway agency, Caltrans, however does not for now allow this option to be considered.

It is important to realize, however, that it was the years-old, detailed analysis of just such an "unrealistic" alternative that provided the blueprint that made it feasible to get rid of San Francisco's other horrendous example of freeway rape along the Embarcadero when the opportunity arose so unexpectedly with the Loma Prieta earthquake. Had that plan and its supporting data not existed, San Francisco's newly recaptured waterfront would still be in the grim shadow of the freeway. That plan, which has proved to be so crucial and prescient for the city, was totally disregarded at the time it was made.

This is perhaps the sharpest difference between the activities of planners and those of architects. In large-scale planning, there is rarely the possibility of quick gratification or the chance to realize an idea while one still remembers why one ever thought it. As one studies the maps of eleven historical milestones, one sees a long chain of dreams, some fulfilled and some not, some that created places of grace and enduring worth, some that were catastrophic. Very few of those ideas, good or bad, were carried to realization by those who conceived them.

After the study of these eleven maps, it is impossible to resist the temptation to offer a gratuitous twelfth one. In the twelfth map, all of the ideas that seem so sensible if one disregards the current politics are combined. The Central Freeway is pulled back; Jacob's Octavia Boulevard extends south and east across Market Street to meet the new freeway touchdown. South Van Ness as conceived by Burnham and the Division of Highways no longer wrecks Eddy's resolution of O'Farrell's grids. Van Ness Avenue ends at Market Street in a major transit atrium, with the possibility of some tall buildings terminating the vista down the street and framing the views of the hills beyond. These tall buildings could resolve the orientations of the two grids that intersect at the site and form a major city landmark. This major development on land reclaimed from roadways would be a fiscal engine to help fund small-scale street improvements throughout

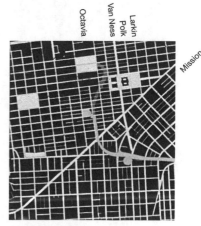

2010 as it might be

143

the district. Just as our small-scale "critical reconstructions" respect but do not replicate the buildings of the nineteenth century, this map finds continuity with the historic city without attempting to thwart the pressures for growth and change that are the life force of cities. This map represents a distillation of ideas about urbanism itself, about the enduring value of the teaching at Cornell, about the implications for other places of the reconstructions in Berlin, about the fundamental insights of Muratori. Perhaps it may someday be useful; that is unknowable.

Surviving Success

One of the great failings of the postwar suburb is that the more of it there is, the less it is like it was supposed to be. Not long after universal mobility is unleashed in a sylvan, bucolic landscape, no one is mobile any longer and the landscape is no longer sylvan or bucolic. This is not a new observation. But what is just now becoming apparent is that, in the unprecedented conditions of the so-called new economy, the best urban places are vulnerable to a similar process of failing by succeeding.

In olden times, there were a very few rich people and, depending upon the society, larger numbers of poor or middle-class people. Not now. There has never been anything quite like the intermittent wealth formation of the new economy. The difference between the new, new rich and the new rich of other generations of technological change is that there are now hordes of them. The sharp, pernicious inequities of the Gold Rush and the industrial revolution are replaced by widespread inequities of a new kind, which are pernicious in a new way. Not only are there now large numbers of people who would be considered truly rich in other times, there is a much vaster multitude of workers in the industries of the new economy who, when times are good, make five times or more what workers in all the other sectors of the economy make. At the height of the last tech boom, a twenty-two-year-old architectural draftsman with some computer skills, making fourteen dollars an hour, could switch professions, call himself an information tech, and make eighty-five dollars an hour. It happened all the time.

To the new, new very rich and their pretty damn rich employees, the failures of the sprawling second-era city are perfectly apparent. They see all the ways that edge cities and postwar suburbs are boring, dysfunctional, and unsatisfying, and in very large numbers, they want no part of them. For the most part, they are smart enough to see the obvious: that New York, San Francisco, Telluride, Aspen, and Jackson Hole are all, in different ways, appealing places to live. Tyson's Corner, Virginia, and Milpitas and Irvine, California, by contrast, are not so hot.

But, *you only hurt the one you love.* New rich techies tote their modems to Telluride because they like to hang with ski bums. But after not so long a while, the new rich techies have bid up the real estate so high that there is hardly a ski bum in sight, except those with trust funds, and you can't find a bartender, a waitress, or a school teacher in town, except when they're working, because most have a two-hour commute. Aspen is the same story, and it is instructive, not because it is unusual or extreme (it is not), but because it is small and therefore understandable. Most of the waiters, bartenders, lift operators, and ski patrol people upon whom the local economy depends cannot afford to live in Aspen and instead live sixty or seventy miles away at the north end of the Aspen Valley. Commute traffic got so bad that the Department of Transportation allocated something like $100 million to widen the road to four lanes for the whole length of the valley, a major environmental and scenic disaster. Common sense, the best existing transit legislation, a New Urbanist mayor, a New Urbanist planning director, and all the king's horses were not enough to switch the highway money into an affordable housing program in the town. A small fraction of the $100 million put into housing would have solved the whole problem *and* made the town a better, more interesting place. Through great efforts, a small amount of affordable housing was eventually built in town, but not nearly enough to forestall the road construction.

On a much vaster scale, the Aspen story is being repeated in economically successful city-regions in many places. As the epicenter of the information economy, the San Francisco Bay Area and San Francisco itself are an egregious and frightening example of a new form of urban sickness. "Sickness" is the right word; when the economy is in one of its manic phases, one senses it in the air and sees evidence of it every day. It dominates conversation as in a town stricken by plague. One day one reads that a group of musicians had been paid $750,000 by their landlord to vacate their space and make way for an Internet company. The next day, the story is that hundreds of doctors and dentists and the city's best pharmacy had been given eviction notices at 450 Sutter Street, a twenty-seven-story Art Deco landmark designed by Timothy Pfleuger. For doctors and dentists, 450 Sutter is the San Francisco equivalent of a Park Avenue address in New York. It is where generations of upper-middle-class kids have stared through Timothy Pflueger's lovely mitred window frames at the view of San Francisco Bay as their teeth got fixed. At one point, before the last economic downturn, it was being taken over at four and a half times its previous rent by an Internet company paying for a lease on the whole building *with a line of credit.*

Eleven percent of the population of San Francisco can afford the city's median-priced house. U.C. Berkeley cannot recruit junior faculty because there is no way to find decent housing on an assistant professor's salary. Stanford is throwing up new housing like in wartime, because graduate students can no longer afford to live off campus. When things are hot, one hears the tales every day: *My kids couldn't afford to live here anymore. My bookkeeper was evicted, had a nervous breakdown, and moved to Idaho. The body shop moved to San Lorenzo. There are no more notary publics around here.* It is not just artists, the poor, and service workers who are intermittently displaced by gentrification— it is also fancy doctors, professors, and well-subsidized grad students. When it had its boom, the Internet economy, fueled by vast amounts of at-risk venture capital, hit the city like a neutron bomb, leaving it physically intact but stripped of the very texture of life that drew people there in the first place.

The next wave of venture capital hysteria may be biotech, or who knows what. In the meantime, there is a sharp real estate recession that is as cruel to some people as the upward spike was to others. The political factionalism and hostilities that these histrionic growth spurts produce is what paralyzes the city and makes large-scale interventions requiring a broad consensus so very difficult. The displaced and their political surrogates *hate* the displacers and theirs. It is not just a matter of policy disagreement; it is true soul-destroying hatred, like in the Balkans or the Middle East.

There was no preparation for this new phenomenon. In the realm of city building, a big problem has to exist for a long time before it is generally perceived how much of a commitment must be made to redress what has gone wrong. By the time the solutions are in place, the damage is vast. The very first topics of planning legislation were responses to the Dickensian horrors of nineteenth-century industrial cities, but they took shape seventy-five years or so after the conditions they addressed were fully formed. New York's New Tenement Law of 1901 mandated light and air for the immigrant housing in the lower East Side, but not until generations had been decimated by tuberculosis. Segregated zoning placed new houses some distance from the smokestacks of Andrew Carnegie's Pittsburgh, a benefit not for the steel workers and coal miners whose toil helped build Chicago and the Union Pacific, but for their grandchildren. In the end, most officials of Beijing may acknowledge that Professor Wu Liangyong was right all along about the need to preserve the city's historic fabric, but there is practically nothing left to preserve. Fifty years after the need became acute, New Urbanism now provides neatly codified practices for the graceful integration of automobiles into cities, but look what automobiles have done to America.

The displacement of the life force of cities, and the tensions caused by displacement, as an inherent feature of a strong and volatile economy are not even recognized as issues in the places that have never experienced them. If you don't happen to live in San Francisco, New York, Seattle, or a choice little place like Telluride, you see displacement as somebody else's local problem, nothing to worry about. It is, in fact, an acute urban problem of the moment. It demands a massive readjustment of priorities and new practices, not yet conceived, that are as radical as the creation of zoning or historic preservation were when they were unknown and desperately needed ideas.

Many things seem to turn up first in San Francisco or very nearby—beatniks and hippies, the antiwar movement, California cuisine, information technology, AIDS care. In the realm of city building, San Francisco also has some firsts. San Francisco didn't invent sprawl or freeways (credit L.A.), but it did have the first freeway revolt, and its citizen activists and real estate industry may have been the first to discover that a nineteenth-century city structure was a better home for life at the end of the twentieth century than the one dreamt of by planners and architects after World War II.

San Francisco has a new first that people in attractive cities everywhere should worry about, if they have not already started. That is paralytic civil strife caused by the tensions of displacement when the beneficiaries of rapid technological change decide for good reason that a particular town is a cool place to be. It is a serious form of failure, and its cause is success.

Out of Town

A distinct kind of architecture has been brought to the world, for better or worse, from Los Angeles, more precisely from that extraordinary little corner of Los Angeles known as Venice, the hang-loose capital of the universe. I once saw a man who perfectly embodied the spirit of the place. He was the only other human in sight on the Venice Beach Boardwalk as I went for a run at dawn. I was trotting southward, and he came northward, a dark-skinned, one-armed East Indian gentleman of late middle age, clad in a turban, tattered shorts, and nothing else, smoking a joint and zipping along on a skateboard with the exquisite, slouchy nonchalance of the supremely skilled. That is the nature of Venice, California, in a single synoptic image: exotic, malformed, excellent at what it tries to be, having fun, but with a certain somber melancholy. His expression made it clear that the wisdom that comes from living for decades on the beach is unlike other forms of wisdom.

Frank Gehry, the grand master, and the movement he helped to unleash in the works of Thom Mayne, Michael Rotundi, Eric Owen Moss, Fred Fisher, Mark Mack, and others are products of Venice. Their work originates deep in the soul of a particular place, like Perrier water, and like Perrier water it is now a global commodity. Los Angeles teaches an architect to survive in, even to revel in, a world that is disjointed, irredeemably ugly to many outsiders, and far beyond the possibility of the normal kind of civic grace that cities have aspired to for as long as cities have existed. It is a world in which invention and iconoclasm are not merely licensed but obligatory.

San Francisco teaches something different. It teaches an architect to believe that the history of urbanism did *not* end a few years ago, that in fact it is still going on, that it demands the same skills that it always has, and that the confusion of the last half of the twentieth century was neither permanent nor inevitable. San Franciscans consider these to be matters of fact because they see in their daily experience how well a city with the qualities of traditional urbanity functions as the setting for contemporary life. They also see the messed-up places in the city and the suburbs built in the last half of the twentieth century, and they are dead certain that these places are not as nice to live, work, shop, or play in as the older parts of San Francisco.

Like Venice, San Francisco is a place with soul, but a different kind of soul. I like to think that my own works are as rooted in my town's *genius loci* as the works of the Venice gang are in theirs. It is natural that an architect who is at home in San Francisco would see the inchoate world of building outside the traditional structure of the city, not as a subject for perverse enjoyment but for reform. It simply makes no sense for a San Franciscan (or a Londoner or a Charlestonian, for that matter) to accept as an imperative of history that the world is destined to be ugly, inconvenient, isolating, disorienting, and without a sense of its own past. One's daily experience shows perfectly clearly that it doesn't *have* to be that way.

The Venice architectural crowd has done an amazing job of exporting building designs all around the world, the spirit of which was conceived in the special circumstance of Los Angeles. Whatever reservations one may have about this form of globalization, it is actually no more sinister an operation than previous forms of colonial architecture that produced the best parts of Singapore, Hong Kong, Tian Jin, Buenos Aires, and Mexico City. Our own work was incubated in San Francisco, and we too are busy trying to build export models, because we are part of the same global economy and information culture as the architects in Venice.

Often when I leave the coherent and comforting urban structure of San Francisco and head out into the suburbs, I feel as if I am visiting the place that Gary Larson depicted in his wonderful cartoon of the Boneless Chicken Farm. As architects and as planners, my colleagues and I bring bones to insert into limp chickens, an activity that one must admit has some things in common with those of colonists, missionaries, and the super-hip architects of Venice, exporting their hometown product around the world. For us, however, the limp chickens that are the focus of our missionary zeal are sad, messy parts of towns that either were always that way or were so completely ravaged in the years after World War II that there was practically nothing left of the physical structure that once made them nice places.

We have had chances to work in sad, messy parts of Los Angeles, and the work we have done there interprets the history and opportunities of that city in a way that is completely different from the work of the Venice architects (one can't quite call them Venetians). For me, it is a twisted reading of Los Angeles to see it as a pastless, placeless *tabula rasa* that can be energized only by heroic feats of eccentricity and weirdness. One can understand that reading, but it has done far more for architectural careers than it has for the continuity of a city that, in many parts, was a much more beautiful and livable place at other times than in the recent past.

An architectural sensibility steeped in belief in the continuity of urban history sees in Los Angeles a past that has not been totally eradicated and that is neither irrelevant nor uninteresting. There is lots of really good stuff there, a whole treasure house of it, if one begins to look—courtyard housing in Hollywood and Pasadena, Craftsman bungalows in Pasadena, the dignified, solid, but long-derelict fabric of downtown that is now beginning to come back, Art Deco exuberance in all its forms, those great fanciful homages to cultures that never really existed—Mission Revival and Spanish Colonial Revival, the early modernism of Schindler, Neutra, and Frank Lloyd Wright—the list can go on and on. The myth of Los Angeles as the place of perpetual newness is just that, a myth, and it is one that threatens a powerful and valuable reality. Aldo Rossi called cities "great encampments of the living and the dead"; urbanism for Rossi had within it a form of ancestor worship. Cities that eradicate themselves in the name of newness—Houston, Singapore, Berlin from 1945 until 1984, most of Beijing—deprive their citizens of some essential form of rooted-ness in the world, rootedness that is like knowing whether it is morning or which way is north.

Urbanism and buildings that root people in the past of a place are not necessarily the same thing as revivalism. Mission Revival, Spanish Colonial Revival, and the architecture of Santa Fe, Santa Barbara, and Disney's Celebration are systematic re-creations of older cultures, real or imagined, as strategies to accomplish the rooting that the architecture of perpetual newness eradicates. It is worth noting, in this regard, that Santa Fe, which now has a totally consistent adobe and ersatz adobe Pueblo-style fabric, was in 1925 a town consisting mostly of painted, wooden Victorian buildings. Today, the new ethnographic museum, no less, is also a wood frame building, clad in Tivex sheets. Over the Tivex is a lumpy layer of sprayed-on urethane foam, then on top of that an elastomeric coating that looks just like adobe rendering after two years of weathering. You can't tell the difference. If in one's youth, one became intoxicated on the powerful ethers of modernism, the same ethers that the architects of Venice emerged from, then one's stomach lacks the enzymes to digest this sort of revivalism, and Santa Fe produces a reflexive nausea.

This nausea is not triggered by some absolute moral position, how-ever, and a simple repeal of modernity through scenographic revival-ism may be workable within what Kenneth Frampton would call "a bounded place-form," like Santa Fe or Santa Barbara. It is, however, totally inconceivable as a strategy for Los Angeles, which poses much more interesting, difficult, and universal questions. The architects and urban-ists held out as models throughout this book see rootedness in time and place as a more complex matter than the fake pueblos of Santa Fe, and it is their works that provide some guidance to the problem of building in Los Angeles.

Our own work in Los Angeles consists of two planning projects and one building complex. The buildings are located right where all the mad pathologies of the postwar American city erupted in 1992 into the largest, longest, and most destructive episode of urban violence in American his-tory. South Central represents the most extreme version of America's pub-lic policy assault on the central city. This was once a stable, physically co-herent community and a decent place for generations of working-class people to raise their families. What is surprising to an outsider visiting South Central for the first time is how well designed, pleasant, and almost desperately well cared for some of it still is, despite the terrifying *Boyz N the Hood* image of it that has been projected around the world.

In 1996, First Interstate Bank, before it was devoured by Wells Fargo, decided that it would be a smart public relations ploy to acquit their obligations under the Community Reinvestment Act by doing something constructive, after four years of highly publicized failed efforts by others in South Central, following the violence of 1992. They selected a site for an architectural competition to build a demonstration project, a site that poignantly embodied much of what had gone wrong with the place through forty years of dreadful public policy.

The site was a long, narrow lot on Vermont Avenue, stretching northward for a block and a half from the corner of 81st street. Vermont Avenue is one of several enormously wide streets that run south from Los Angeles through the ghetto communities of South Central, Compton, and Watts. During the 1940s, hundreds of thousands of southern blacks were drawn here to work in the Kaiser and Fontana steel mills, the Goodyear Tire and Rubber Company, Hughes Aircraft, and scores of other industries that helped America to outproduce the Axis powers and win the war. Vermont Avenue had a trolley line in the middle of the street then and was lined with a solid strip of small businesses, bars, nightclubs, restaurants, churches, and institutions that served the residential neighborhoods to the east and west.

Pictures of Vermont Avenue in the 1940s look a lot like the cherished, flourishing streetcar streets of Toronto look today. But unlike those lovely streets in Toronto, Vermont Avenue was situated within the urban history of the United States, not that of Canada. What I first visited in 1996 was the result of trade policies, highway programs, and racial politics that Mike Davis documents with such compelling bitterness in his monumental book *The City of Quartz*. It was a scene of total devastation and abandonment, equaled in my experience only by similar parts of Detroit and St. Louis and not equaled by the bombed-out sections of East Berlin in the 1950s. Most of the buildings along Vermont had completely vanished, without leaving the smallest archeological trace to record the life they once housed. I drove along block after block of vacant lots with a few scattered buildings, many boarded up, some occupied by enterprising souls such as Million Article Thompson, who treaded water on the sea of abandonment by selling used hardware and plumbing fixtures and providing divorce counseling, tax preparation, notary services, and vacuum cleaner repair.

One block west of Vermont and 81st, a pair of palm trees marks the entrance to an astonishingly handsome working-class residential neighborhood known as Vermont Knolls. It would be hard to find anyplace in America where the lawns are more neatly manicured, the houses better painted, the cars more polished, and the children more polite or better groomed than in Vermont Knolls. Jobs, shopping, services—almost everything the people of Vermont Knolls need for their daily life, except their churches—are now far, far away, but amid the abandonment, this modest African American community holds on as a bastion of bourgeois propriety and civility. Across Vermont on the other side is a residential neighborhood of a completely different sort, a squalid, scary mess of a place, with *Boyz N the Hood* types much in evidence. The east side of the street helps explain the obsessive propriety on the west side of Vermont.

On the corner of the competition site itself, one building remained, a tattered but once splendid Art Deco edifice with a celebratory tower on top that had been built as a market hall in 1931 and had more recently served as an administration building for Peppardine College, before that conservative institution abandoned South Central for the less challenging environs of Malibu. The next building down the street was a block and a half away at the other end of the site, an impeccably maintained little white church with a steeple.

The professional advisor to the competition prevailed upon us to enter the competition, and we were selected as architects for one of the competing architect/developer/contractor teams. Our developer and our contractor had both grown up in South Central. Each of the teams was expected to meet several times with people from the community at the huge, spotless campus of the Crenshaw Christian Center, just north of the site. From our new partners, and from this series of meetings, we got a taste of the anger, hopelessness, and mistrust bred by the systematic destruction of the heart of this community.

The most heart-rending moment came on the morning we met

with the dynamic young city councilman from South Central, Mark Ridley Thomas, at his Vermont Avenue office. The councilman had announced that on this morning, his office would accept applications for two hundred jobs as janitors at Los Angeles International Airport, which is not far away. When we arrived to meet with Thomas, we walked past a line of several thousand African American men and women of all ages, three or four abreast, stretched all around the long block. Most seemed to be dressed in the clothes they wore to church, and all whom we talked to seemed far too articulate and well educated to be competing at one-in-fifty odds to be selected as a janitorial candidate, but there they were. It put our own competition in an odd perspective, and it forced upon us the question of what, if anything, did we bring that is of any value in this terrible circumstance of American urban history?

The loudest, most emphatic message we heard from the people of Vermont Knolls was one that could be heard in any middle-class neighborhood in America: NO SUBSIDIZED RENTAL HOUSING; NO LOW-INCOME PEOPLE. Put the poor folks in Beverly Hills, they said, South Central had enough. The bank should go stuff their CRA obligations in somebody else's backyard. Almost anywhere else, these sentiments would have seemed reprehensible and to be resisted, but not here. The toehold on a decent life that these people clung to was so tenuous, so palpably threatened. Their efforts to maintain a place of pride and respectability in the face of all that had been done to them seemed so just that one had to listen.

The goal of the competition was to provide some kind of development prototype for the hundreds of blocks of vacant land with commercial zoning in South Central. Obviously, in the era of the freeway and the power center, these abandoned places were not going to come back as the rows of neighborhood stores that had thrived with streetcars in the 1940s. What we designed for Vermont Village Plaza (named by Councilman Thomas) is ownership housing, subsidized for working families, so that a new house cost about the same as one in Vermont Knolls. Interspersed between the houses along Vermont are small retail spaces. Since most homebuyers would be two-income families and because in L.A. two jobs requires two cars, each house had to have two secure parking spaces, especially secure because the neighborhood was so dangerous.

Vermont Avenue is enormous, eight lanes wide with a median and

Vermont Village Plaza, courtyard

two-lane frontage roads on either side. We knew that our architecture with its modest program of houses and stores would have to stand up to the scale of this huge street and the many abandoned lots along it. We therefore made the architecture as heroic as our modest program and budget would permit. The townhouses are organized in groups of four, over stores, with garages tucked out of site. Between each group of four is a small cobbled street that leads to a group of houses in the midblock. Spanning each little street is a bridge that forms a portal and serves as a pair of decks for the houses that don't have private gardens. Marching down the block is a giant order of three-story pilasters, vaguely derived from the decorative scheme of the Art Deco monument on the corner.

At the center of it all is a courtyard with a trellised loggia around it and four large palm trees. It is intended as an evocation of those courtyards in Hollywood and Pasadena that are so much a part of the enduring myth of Edenic Southern California. Finally, this secure compound has to look friendly and welcoming, and the gates that make it safe are discreetly placed at the back of openings. Amazingly, when one visits Ver-

Vermont Village Plaza, streetscape

mont Village Plaza now, one usually sees actual pedestrians, something almost inconceivable before it was built.

I know that Vermont Village Plaza is well regarded in the neighborhood and that its residents take great pride in it. Many of them had witnessed the forces of history turning a place that had stimulated affection and identity into a featureless no-place. What I hope our project provides is some combination of hope and memory for people who had been stripped of both. If it succeeds in this, then that success comes from a reading of urban history that one acquires more easily as a student of a place like San Francisco, which values its own past, than one does as a student of the architects of Venice and their seductive culture of eternal invention.

Gemeindebauen

When Vermont Village Plaza was under construction in 1997, we received another, much larger commission that was similar in many ways. Vermont Village Plaza applies lessons learned about urbanism in San Francisco to the urban history of Los Angeles, and its younger brother in San Jose, our mixed-use block known as 101 San Fernando, does something similar for that town. It should be obvious, however, to people who keep track of this sort of thing that these siblings are also grandchildren of housing and block designs that are not in San Francisco but were conceived and built in Vienna in the 1920s and early 1930s.

When I first saw them more than forty years ago, I thought there was something especially magnificent about the great Viennese complexes of social housing built in the years after World War I. As a nineteen-year-old student I knew nothing about housing, architecture, or urbanism, but you don't have to be a musicologist to like Mozart. When something is really good, it's easy to tell. The images of these places have haunted me ever since, and traces of them have appeared and reappeared in my own work, more or less consciously, ever since I have had opportunities to design little chunks of urban infill. The superlative recent book *The Architecture of Red Vienna*, by Eva Blau, tells why these seventy-five-year-old works should stick in someone's mind so tenaciously and seem so important today.

Eva Blau explains that the little-known architects for these housing blocks were the superbly trained students of the largest giant in my personal pantheon of architectural heroes, Otto Wagner. For a variety of fascinating reasons, the Marxist Social Democrats of Vienna rejected the architectural avant-garde of the day and turned to another kind of modern architect for their massive and politically radical housing program. It is interesting to note that *The Architecture of Red Vienna* is something of a revisionist history. From Sigfried Giedion in the 1920s to Manfredo Tafuri in the 1970s, modernist academic critics were dismissive of the Viennese accomplishment, considering it a compromised vision and a failure to achieve true modernity.

Nonetheless, Wagner considered himself a progressive innovator who embraced the technological changes and huge infrastructure projects of his time with zeal. His transportation planning, his magnificent waterworks, and his exquisite subway stations, which are rivaled only by Moscow's, remade the face of Vienna. But Wagner was also a classicist par excellence and, like others trained in the late nineteenth century, was a master of ornament, composition, and draftsmanship. He crossed the threshold of the twentieth century eagerly and optimistically, but he was armed with the full complement of nineteenth-century weapons.

The great accomplishments of Red Vienna are due in large part to the fact that Wagner's gifts as a teacher equaled his achievements as an architect and urbanist. Wagner, the imperial architect, died miserably of influenza and malnutrition seven weeks before the armistice. In 1919, when the Social Democrats of Vienna began the monumental undertaking of building a new society on the rubble of the Hapsburg Empire, there existed a large cadre of *Wagnerschuler*, who inherited the essential traits of their teacher. They were progressive innovators who also understood and loved the heritage of their own city. They were modernists who had also mastered classical composition and ornament. They were social architects who were also formalists. They were architects of splendid individual buildings who were also urbanists and whose buildings served a larger order of things.

Austro-Marxism was a cultural program as much as an economic one; in the 1920s it was politically essential that the new industrial proletariat be housed in a way that made its citizens a part of the splendors of the historic city, and not just housed but celebrated and memorialized. For these reasons, and because the Social Democrats controlled only the city itself, not the surrounding countryside, modernist housing blocks on the German suburban *Zeilenbau* model would not do for the postwar city/state. That form of decentralized city, with its idealized rows of mass-produced slab blocks facing the sun, was brought to America by architects, most notably Oscar Stonorov, who sculpted the bust of Catherine Bauer that I measured in Bill Wheaton's office. The *Zeilenbau* housing type, which would later become *de rigueur* during the Gropius regime at Harvard and under Mies van der Rohe and Ludwig Hilbersheimer at the Illinois Institute of Technology, would not solve the housing crises or the political problems the Viennese Social Democrats faced after the Great War. The Viennese Social Democrats and their architects anticipated the terrible fate of the German *Zeilenbau* housing model long before it was exported to the United States, the Soviet Union, China, and everywhere else. The Viennese architects and their political patrons knew that it was necessary for Viennese worker housing to join the classical city, to be as grand as the classical city, and for its residents to live lives that were not culturally or physically inferior to those of the bourgeoisie. They invented the *Gemeindebau* as a building type that served these ends.

As Eva Blau's book has now made clear to me, my own affinity for the Viennese housing blocks comes from their success at achieving exactly what we have been attempting to build in our own work for decades: housing fabric as urban reconstruction; housing fabric in the center of town, where it is accessible to jobs, services, and the culture of the city; housing fabric that blurs the separations of class, race, and age; housing fabric of sufficient grandeur that it is a source of pride and identity for its residents.

Moreover, the architects of Red Vienna had budgets, really difficult and constraining budgets. Collectively, they worked out inexpensive, normative building practices, and then they all worked within those conventions. They faced the same problems we face today: economic upheaval, uprootedness, the need to build cheaply, and radical change in scale. They solved all of our problems, brilliantly and massively, and we have just to look at how they did it. The same formal strategies that served the *Waqnerschuler* in 1925 Vienna work for us seventy-five years later. The permeable perimeter block that my colleagues and I build whenever we get the chance is basically a Viennese Hof, slightly modified to accommodate automobiles. The Gemeindebau is also a traditional Hof, altered to accommodate the social programs and the huge scale of Red Vienna'a housing program.

One trait that the Vienna of 1919–34 and the San Jose of 1975–2001 had in common was a large-scale economic upheaval that caused a radical change in the size of buildings in the city center. San Jose was a sleepy and decrepit suburban town that suddenly found itself at the center of world's most important new industry, the very engine of globalization. Our 101 San Fernando was built to house Silicon Valley tech workers—some at market rate, 20 percent in subsidized units—in San Jose's newly dense and intensively developed downtown. The scale of housing needs in Vienna corresponded to a similar upheaval, and individual housing estates frequently covered several blocks in a city fabric where historic blocks were typically comprised of multiple buildings by different hands over time.

In their best moments, the *Wagnerschuler* did two things simultaneously to give measure to their large new buildings and to make them fit harmoniously with the smaller old buildings. First, they emphasized and decorated small domestic details—balcony rails, planter boxes, small windows for kitchens and baths. Their decorative schemes did not mimic the too expensive and unreproducible detail of historic buildings but did provide a *density* of detail so that the play of light across their facades was similar to the older buildings. But they did not stop at coziness. They took from the classical strains of their master the ability to give grandeur and measure to their big blocks with giant orders of pilasters and multistory portals through them. Wagner gave them the skills to use the scaling strategies of the Renaissance through an inventive, thoroughly modern system of ornament. Their giant pilasters and portals have no classical ornament, but they do the same job of giving measure to large facades as do those of Michelangelo, Palladio, or Scamozzi. The fit between the political intentions of these radical social housing projects and their combination of domesticity and grandeur was completely apt.

101 plays a similar formal game. It occupies two-thirds of an oversized city block, the rest of which is small Mission Revival or Craftsman-style buildings from the teens and twenties, some of them quite embellished and

101 San Fernando, streetview

handsome. It also must deal with the presence all along its eastern flank of three very large, expensive modernist public buildings, including the new San Jose City Hall by Richard Meier. The urbanistic role of 101 is to repair the city fabric, help provide a setting for City Hall, and mediate between these very different kinds of buildings so that the whole ensemble is coherent. And it must do this within the normal constraints of craft and budget that apply to ordinary rental apartment buildings in contemporary California: stucco wall surfaces, thin metal windows that are only slightly recessed, a bit of embellishment in the form of balconies or awnings.

The unavoidably thin and flat stucco walls of 101 have a whole layer of light metal exedra casting shadows across them—balconies, arcades, sunshades, lightposts, privacy screens, trellises. The detailing of this metal falls within the budget and craft skills of a low-bid fabricator; it is decidedly modernist in character but matches, more or less, the density of detail of the historic buildings. The unit plans themselves are shaped to create little rooms—kitchens or studies—that stack on one another and form

101 San Fernando, court and portal

a giant order of five-story pilasters that march all around the three block faces of the building. This helps give the humble apartment building a scale of sufficient grandeur that is a comfortable companion to the big, new public buildings across the street.

Finally, like Schmid and Aichinger's seminal Fuchsenfeldhof and many Gemeindebauen that followed its model, 101 is penetrated by giant portals, three and a half stories high, down the two long sides of the block. In Vienna, the midblocks of large projects became networks of pedestrian spaces containing an array of social services—workshops, gyms, classrooms, and retail shops—connected to the surrounding streets by portals through the perimeter block. Our 101 has the perimeter block, the portals, and the pedestrian passages, but unfortunately in this speculative rental building, not such an interesting and diverse program within. Our pedestrian ways are lined with unit entrances, we have retail and a gym facing the street, and the midblock lanes do lead to a recreation facility, but our means of providing housing through the speculation of private developers cannot provide renters with the social services of Red Vienna. Same intentions, different system, different time.

Perhaps the mediations of old and new, large and small, and the manipulations of cheap and normative construction methods in our building will be met with the same dismissiveness as the works of Red Vienna that I admire so deeply. 101 does not attempt to break new ground programatically or in the techniques of building. Perhaps it too will be seen as a failure to achieve modernity. What it does do is find meaning in architecture as urbanism, as a spatial construct that is an essential part of something larger and more important than itself. If it has a fraction of the enduring value for its city and for its inhabitants as the masterworks of the *Wagnerschuler*, I will one day have a proud and happy ghost.

PART 5

IN ASIA

Undervaluing what one has and coveting what one doesn't have is a common human trait—one might say a weakness. It frequently wrecks marriages and causes people to trade in perfectly serviceable and attractive automobiles. The process of coveting and appropriating has always gone on, sometimes in destructive ways, sometimes in ways that are innocent or healthy. I like to think of the use of an old Viennese housing model for San Jose as healthy appropriation. But global information culture gives pace and scale to the process of appropriation that it has never had before, and it is a process that can destroy more than it creates.

Architects and urbanists who have lived through the enthusiasms and experiments of the last half of the twentieth century in America and Western Europe see that much of Asia seems absolutely determined to repeat the urban history of the West, including its most egregious and obvious mistakes. Many Asian planners, developers, and bureaucrats also seem indifferent to the characteristics of their own cities that have emanated spontaneously from Asian culture for millennia. The very qualities that Western visitors envy and cherish mean little to many Asian people, who associate them with overcrowding, poverty, and a political, economic, and military history they are striving with all their mighty energy to escape.

The desolate new suburbs of Beijing are similar to those postwar Italian edge-city landscapes that so fascinated and repelled Federico Fellini. Big trucks roar by the scraggly no-man's lands that surround row after row of stacked concrete apartments. As in so many Fellini films, life asserts itself, pathetically but doggedly, no matter how bleak the setting. In these new suburbs, one sees from time to time places where something like the mercantile street life of old Beijing has spontaneously reestablished itself in abandoned or temporary buildings on the edges of vast housing projects. Embarrassed developers and bureaucrats are quick to explain that the spontaneous markets will all be torn down as soon as the air-conditioned mall gets built.

For some Westerners, the most dramatic Asian transformations are thrilling. After a three-year posting as French consul general and director of the French Cultural Mission in Shanghai, Nicholas Chapuis went into culture shock at his next posting as director of the French Institute and Embassy of Cultural Affairs in London. For Chapuis, London had become "Third World" and all of Europe "a Disneyland of castles and good living." London was just so *slow*. It shocked him to see that two full years into the twenty-first century, lots of Londoners didn't even have cell phones, and that when Broadband went down for two hours in the middle of a working day, people didn't seem to mind or even notice. This would have been unthinkable in Shanghai, where the action is, and where action doesn't have much to do with the love of antiquities or with good living.

There is no question that the optimism, pace of change, and sheer power of economic force unleashed in Asia are overwhelmingly seductive —as modernity and modernism have always been. Perhaps if one experiences their Asian manifestations only intermittently and not too deeply, one is in a better position not to be seduced, and to hear those few Asian voices who ask whether history has really ordained that it all has to become what it is so rapidly becoming. The essays that follow are travel sketches, the views of an outsider witnessing the fifty years of urban history that we have just lived through in the West rerun at much higher speed on a larger screen.

Dorothy Lamour on a Flying Pigeon

In 1997, 45 percent of the population of Shanghai still lived at incredible densities along tiny alleys in districts built around the turn of the century. In these districts there was no plumbing, and for many residents quarters were too cramped to cook indoors. The little streets, eight or nine feet wide, were filled with the sights and smells of the fabulous local cuisine in all stages of preparation and consumption: baskets of reddish live eels in several varieties; piles of bright yellow melons; live chickens and ducks in wooden cages and their newly departed brethren hanging in rows; people chopping, simmering, stir-frying all manner of stuff; and families eating right there on the street.

Amazingly, in these primitive and jammed conditions, sewerage smells were rare, and most children looked neat, healthy, and well cared for. It was not uncommon to see an absolutely smashing, exquisitely groomed young woman, totally decked out in forties retro style—lacquered hair piled to the sides, flawless red nails and lipstick, platform wedgies, shoulder pads, and layer upon layer of chiffon—emerge from a one-room hovel with six occupants. Off she pedaled, dodging potholes and four generations of people on that indestructible human-powered relic of Mao's China, the Flying Pigeon. After all the years of chopped hair, neighbor spying on neighbor, and unspeakable punishments for "bourgeois tendencies," femininity returned with a vengeance from exactly the point it was abandoned in 1949. Hedy Lamar, Gene Tierney, Barbara Stanwyck, Dorothy Lamour—all there, everywhere you looked.

The old districts with the alleys were being razed so quickly that most are now gone, replaced by the new high-rises and widely spaced mid-rises stretching into the smog, farther than you can see. The soulless blanket of *Zeilenbau* slabs that Glasgow and Brussels and other places have now begun to eliminate is being replaced a thousandfold in Shanghai. And not surprisingly, the people still in the alleys can hardly wait for their own new apartments, where they can eat indoors, hang their clothes, and wash themselves. Perhaps it is only to an outsider who takes those things for granted that the disappearance of the life of the street seems so tragic.

The Diagram

For decades, students of architecture drew the same little diagram. They drew it under Gropius at Harvard, under Mies van der Rohe and Ludwig Hilbersheimer at the Illinois Institute of Technology, and at dozens of other schools that mimicked those great temples of modernism. It is a diagram that relates the height of buildings and the spaces between them to the angle of the sun at the winter solstice. It was this little drawing more than anything else that shaped the generation of American public housing that was started at the end of the 1930s, was built for forty years or so, and is now being torn down. This diagram presented an argument about health, hygiene, and well-being for people moving out of the insalubrious slums of American cities. It resulted in rows and rows of identical buildings all facing the sun, like so many morning glories and spaced at just that optimum distance dictated by the azimuth of the sun and the height of windowsills. It was what Mel Scott and T. J. Kent were thinking about when they put forth their *New City* plan for San Francisco in 1948.

It was not until Jane Jacobs published her great testament to common sense, *The Death and Life of Great American Cities*, in 1961 that anyone really wrote anything cogent about how simplistic, monomaniacal, and fundamentally crazy this diagram really was. In her grandmotherly wisdom, Jane Jacobs told us all what we already really knew: that life is far more complex than sun diagrams, and that real cities like New York and Paris are not made by simple little formulas. The story of the brutal, soul-destroying places that most of that public housing became does

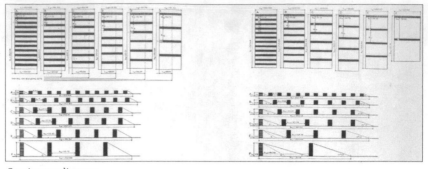

Gropius sun diagram

not need to be retold. As is now understood by those who know best about solar things, even the sun is more complex than the old Gropius sun diagrams.

It would be nice to say that the world has made progress since the bad old times when those New Cities and horrible public housing projects were laid out according to the azimuth of the sun. One could say that only if one has not been to China in the last ten years or so. It is hard for people in the West to understand the power that the Gropius sun diagram has for people who have been living six or eight to a room, without plumbing, on streets ten feet wide. In our lifetimes, most of us have never experienced, seen, or imagined overcrowding as it has existed for hundreds of millions of Chinese. To grasp what is now occurring in China, one must add the sun diagram to a few other irresistible new attractions, including a five- to tenfold increase in space per person, indoor plumbing, washing machines, television, air-conditioning, computer games, the Internet and, for many people, private automobiles. What one then has is a transformation of city life that is at least as radical as the difference between the politics and styles of the Cultural Revolution of the 1970s and the wild consumer capitalism of the Chinese present.

Consider two typical households in present-day Shanghai. Each consists of a family of three; one lives in an old neighborhood that has not yet been torn down, the other in an apartment that is six years old. The old place faces right onto a little street and is both a dwelling and a home for the family businesses: a hair salon and a store that sells cooking oil and woks. Its approximate dimensions are ten by fourteen feet, and by necessity the family does laundry, hangs it to dry, prepares and cooks food, and has meals on the sidewalk along with everybody else on the street. In summer, it is very hot and much nicer to be outside. In winter when it is cold, some of the activities of the street—mainly eating—retreat indoors, but food preparation and laundry still go on outside.

The other household is on the sixteenth floor in a cluster of new high-rises, where not only is there no street life, there are no streets, only deserted spaces between buildings with some grass and places to park bicycles. The apartment contains all of the same activities as the old one, including a home business. The man of the house is Mr. Shen, who works as a conservator of paintings in the Shanghai Museum. At home, his dining room functions as a workshop where he does restoration work and mounts art in the traditional ways for private clients. Also in the dining room is a brand-new computer, where the teenage son and his buddy play computer games endlessly; in the kitchen, there is a large color television set. The living room faces south and has a nice terrace with laundry hanging to dry. The Shens like their washing machine but don't want a dryer, which they consider unsanitary and bad for clothing.

Old neighborhoods in Shanghai are being torn down at a rate of 3.6 million square meters per year. New housing is being put up at a rate of 200,000 units per year, and that is just in Shanghai—the national figure is something like 12 million units per year. China's housing program is, by any measure, the largest construction project in human history. All, or virtually all, of this incredible enterprise is given its essential form by that all-pervasive little diagram of the sun that architecture students drew so obsessively for decades. Chinese housing is so slavishly devoted to solar orientation that almost all of the units are flats with two exposures, regardless of any circulation inefficiencies or fire safety problems that this creates. Because they are willing for the sake of the sun to have stairs and elevators that serve only two units per floor, and willing not to have two fire exits for high-rise units, all of the flats can run all the way through the building and orient south. With no north-facing units to worry about, they twist the Gropius diagram ninety degrees and make all buildings run within fifteen degrees of east/west. Despite the twist, the idea is the same but even more monomaniacal than the German *Zeilenbauen*, which so influenced American public housing. The China experience is American urban renewal and public housing of the fifties and sixties multiplied a millionfold. They are doing just what we did, but lots more of it, for more compelling versions of the same reasons.

We discovered late, but not too late, what was wrong with that simplistic diagram. With the help of Jane Jacobs, Colin Rowe, Aldo Rossi, the brothers Krier, and others, we learned that the town is as important as the house. We learned why the spaces that make towns—the towns we love and go to whenever we get the chance—cannot be made by sun diagrams, at least not the kind of sun diagrams that China has turned into the world's most inflexible building codes.

According to the Beijing Building Code, the azimuth of the sun in winter is thirty-six degrees and the space between buildings must be not less than 1.6 times the height of the buildings. In what little is left of Beijing's traditional fabric of courtyard houses and hutongs (residential lanes), the height-to-width ratio of the courts and lanes is typically 1.5 or 2.5 to 1, *not* 1 to 1.6. In Italy, traditional urban fabric typically has a height to width of at least 2 to 1, and 4 to 1 is not uncommon. Most people, even die-hard modernists or Chinese housing bureaucrats, can agree that the traditional urban fabric in most of Italy is pretty nice—and not just to walk through, but to live in.

What made the Hutongs of Beijing uninhabitable was not their proportions; it was the overcrowding they were subjected to after private property began to be expropriated in 1949. Homeowners who survived the revolution and did not flee had other families assigned to share their houses, eight families, ten families, or more crammed into what had been a decent house for a single family. Is it any wonder that people who now have lived for decades with all those others in a house that is falling apart, without the least modicum of privacy, without indoor plumbing, refrigeration, or closets, would now welcome a shiny, new, private three-bedroom flat with all of that and more? Amid this completely novel circumstance of *owning* what they have dreamt of for so long, one could not expect many to notice that something is missing or to complain about it.

This story is not a new story, nor is it unique to China. But after so much new building, there are now stirrings in China, just as there were stirrings in Europe after it dawned on people what modernist postwar reconstruction was really like, just as there were stirrings in the United States after urban renewal got rolling in the 1960s. Jacques Tati's prescient and brilliant 1958 film, *Mon Oncle,* foreshadowed the architectural movement *Tendenza,* which rediscovered the principles, the traditions, and the value of European urbanism ten years later. Jane Jacobs wrote *The Death and Life of Great American Cities* in 1961, but the juggernaut of urban renewal was not knocked off its rails until the end of the 1960s, and her message did not really take shape in new building practices for another decade after that.

China is now in a similar position to Western Europe in 1958. A vast amount of new construction has been built to satisfy a desperate need, after a long, long time in which virtually nothing was built. And that new construction is almost all shaped by the same conventions and beliefs that shaped much of the reconstruction of Europe. In China, the orthodoxy of the sun diagram is more rigid than it ever was in Europe, and there have been fewer heretics and nonbelievers in a regime that does not exactly embrace dissent. But there are just now the first stirrings of criticism of what has been accomplished with such amazing energy.

The beautiful film *Shower* by the Chinese director Zhang Yang is their equivalent of *Mon Oncle.* Its story centers on an old bathhouse on a Beijing hutong. Old men and a few young ones go to the bathhouse everyday, and some of them spend all day there. For the old man who runs the bathhouse, his retarded son, and their patrons, the bathhouse and its companionship are their life. The bathhouse, and the traditional neighborhood of which it is part, is about to be torn down, and the men of the bathhouse will be dispersed to new places where the apartments will all have bathrooms and there will be no bathhouses.

A sentimental movie about the life of the hutongs would probably not have been made five years ago and would not have had an audience, but *Shower* was a moderate hit. Five years ago there were no books on the hutongs, but now there is an exquisite one that is sold all over Beijing. In a brilliant strategic move, one of those in Beijing who mourned the loss of the hutongs had the insight to start a pedicab company catering to international tourists, reasoning that if the traditional fabric of the city became a tourist attraction, the authorities might have some interest in preserving some of it. In a modest way at least, the strategy is working, and China's fledgling historic preservation movement now directs its attention to city fabric as well as to monuments. The prescient, heroic work of Professor Wu at last is officially recognized. It takes time for cultural rumblings like these to coalesce into a way of doing things, a way that is sufficiently formulated to challenge a juggernaut like the one rolling out those Chinese slab blocks by the mile.

Colin Rowe, because he was an academic who spent all of his adult life surrounded by academic architects, also spent much of his life being annoyed and amused by a phenomenon he saw every day: the cocksure conviction among his colleagues that history was on their side, that they were riding the tide of dialectics to certain victory. If he had been a different kind of fellow leading a different kind of life, he might have discovered the same phenomenon among Communist Party apparatchiks, or Nazis, or real estate developers.

It is really developers more than anyone who place their bets on the inevitability of historic process. "This is the way things are," they say. "This is the way the market works." The fact that markets change all the time, that people go broke all the time when things change, does not seem to rattle the belief in conventions that guides the decisions of most (but not all) developers. So most (but not all) build malls because malls are the way things are. Then Starbuck's, Pottery Barn, and millions of Americans rediscover main streets, and malls go bust by the tens of thousands. The Chinese developers who build those tarted-up Soviet slab blocks set exactly 1.6 times their height apart according to the old Gropius sun diagram believe to the center of their bones that they are designed by history itself and that there is no alternative. Sometime, not soon, but sometime they will find themselves holding a large empty bag as millions upon millions of Chinese remember what it was that they had and what it is that they lost.

Mao tried to suppress the Chinese spirit of enterprise, and now just a few years after his death, one cannot find even a trace of that brief, dour episode. Along the Bund on Shanghai's waterfront stands a large statue of Mao. He looks out at the dazzling new neon of multinational corporations, the hundred-story towers in Pudong, the flashy new cable-stay bridges that span the river, and the crowds of stylish people, women especially, who swirl around him. One can only describe his expression as that of be-wilderment at the reemergence of the mercantile zest of his people.

The sociability of the street is also wired in their genes, and we can safely bet they will not forget it for long.

The Prosperity Bomb

Imagine a change more radical than replacement of the horse with the automobile. Imagine a century compressed into ten years. Imagine something that has never occurred before—a complex and ancient society suddenly choosing to replace itself with a new culture learned from television. Imagine a place where cars were a rarity until recently suddenly overrun with millions of them. Imagine cars imported at a thousand times the rate that roads can be built. Imagine masses of peasants whose ancestors were peasants for three millennia but whose children are suburban yuppies. Imagine thousand-year-old cities tripling in size in the course of a few years. Imagine the largest international investment fund you ever imagined.

In 1985, it may have been permissible to say these things were speculations—scary perhaps, but only speculations, possible outcomes. Now that is no longer so. Each of these imaginings came to pass, suddenly, massively, and without the hiatus of war or depression in which to dream, to plan, to get ready for the change to come. In Indonesia, there was no polemic to lay the groundwork for this change, no policies to build infrastructure, no period of anticipation to build cultural readiness. The polycentric, auto-dominated, pastless, cultureless North American megalopolis descended on the ancient cities of Java like a virus for which there are no antibodies. The conquest was instantaneous and total. People who wanted to plan for these events were like athletes who missed training camp. Play yourself into shape during the games that count.

In the intermittent cataclysm of prosperity that has befallen Indonesia, there is an overwhelming desire among developers, marketers, and public officials to mimic the forms of American suburbia. They yearn to build the shopping malls, subdivisions, business parks, and freeways that, to many, represent deliverance from a past for which they feel the inverse of nostalgia. The planning and design firms that built California's Orange County find an eager market for their services in Indonesia, and they happily deliver "product," brewed to exactly the same formula they use at home, just like Coca-Cola or McDonald's.

The sponsors and patrons of vast new projects, those who stand to profit from them, do not want to hear that the benefits of American-style suburbia may not be sustainable, that it may contain the seeds of its own destruction within it, that even in its place of origin it is not always a satisfactory city form or way of life.

It is not merely hard, it is completely impossible to convince private Indonesian developers that town planning that segregates classes and reinforces class differences undermines the political stability upon which they depend. The American debacle of race and class, and its relationship to suburbanization, highway construction, subsidies of the automobile, and the decanting of cities, has no meaning whatsoever to Indonesian developers, for whom separation of the middle class and the lower class is an essential component of their new ethos of marketing.

Part of that separation, probably the most disastrous part, is the identification of public transportation with the lower classes and the automobile with the new middle class. They simply do not see how massive and how devastating the impact of the automobile will be, and the degree to which the system of roads and streets that worked fine for the many decades when the car was an elite conveyance will be completely overwhelmed when a huge, new middle class drives.

These developers and officials cannot understand or accept what we have learned about America from our own life experience, and they proudly serve us food from McDonald's to show that they are progressive and prosperous. It is conversely as hard for us to accept the idea that people rooted in ancient histories see no value either in their indigenous past or in the frequent grace of their Dutch colonial past. They routinely discard and demolish artifacts, architecture, districts and towns, a legacy of centuries, like useless junk.

In 1994, during the headiest days of Indonesian growth and international investment, our firm and that of Peter Calthorpe were asked by one of the largest Indonesian developers to join forces for an invited international competition to prepare master plans for two new towns, one outside Jakarta and the other outside of Suribaya in eastern Java. We won the competition and over the next two years prepared detailed versions of the two master plans. Very large plans like these tend not to survive political and economic upheaval, and ours appear to be so fated, though, like many town plans of the past, they may be dusted off at the next turning of the wheel of fortune.

The plans did provide an opportunity to confront the meaning of globalization in its most direct and tangible forms, and to try to figure out practical ways to accept its benefits and its inevitability while trying to blunt its grossness. We were blessed in this undertaking by knowing a gifted young Indonesian planner, Wijac Sarosa, who was at Berkeley finishing his Ph.D. Wijac had worked for our developer client but shared our general views about things. He helped us through the competition and then became our guide to what we could and should do and to what stood a chance of being accepted.

The main ideas of our plans came from what Wijac taught us. Instead of the formless sprawl of the American-planned Javanese "new towns" that we visited, our plans are based on the traditional structure of Javanese settlements. In these older settlements, there is a clear organization of municipal government and services and a correspondingly clear and coherent physical structure. The smallest unit of community is called the RW (pronounced "airway"), a group of houses constituting a neighborhood. Several RWs cluster to form an RT ("airtay") or village. The RT has a mosque, sometimes a store, a village green, and a council composed of representatives of the RWs. Several RTs form a Kelurahan, which has a center containing stores, a school, and municipal services.

Our plans are literal, physical expressions of this hierarchy, with the public buildings, markets, and open spaces of each Kelurahan providing the opportunity for a little piece of civic design. Some things about the plans, such as the hierarchy of RT, RW, and Kelurahan, are strictly Indonesian. Other things come from our own practice and American experience. For instance, we did not think that the markets in each Kelurahan could be sustained only by their own population. Accordingly, each Kelurahan is located on an arterial road, and as per good New Urbanist practice, the markets have a parking lot side on the arterial and a pedestrian side facing the main public square of the Kelurahan. This combination of pedestrian/civic space and automobile-based distribution of goods is different from the Orange County model in the other new towns, which have only automobile access to shopping malls.

From the earliest times to the present, it has been axiomatic in Indonesian towns large and small for commerce to be on the main street. This is true in the smallest village and in Jakarta, a city of 16 million. Imagine the largest skyscrapers in New York and its main and only traffic arterial occupying the same space, and you get a picture of Jakarta's congestion. To deal with the inevitable congestion that two-car households would cause in our new towns, we argued that our plans needed two kinds of roads: large, fast ones dedicated to the commute traffic to Jakarta and Suribaya, respectively, and smaller market roads that connected the Kelurahans, provided the location for the traditional fabric of shop houses, and provided places for open spaces where the vendors of the informal markets could gather. Wherever the market roads enters a Kelurahan, it breaks into two smaller one-way roads, each congenial to pedestrians. The plans apply these ideas to two different settings: one in abandoned rice fields near Jakarta and the other interwoven through existing settlements near Suribaya. A main idea we put forth for the Bumi Jaya Plan near Suribaya was that the developers would *not* buy out the existing settlements and tear them down, as had been their intention. Our plan attempted to demonstrate that new and old could coexist and that a certain amount of class integration was possible and marketable.

All of this was going along reasonably well, with construction started outside Jakarta, when the tsunami of 1997 hit the Indonesian economy. The last we heard about Puri Jaya and Bumi Jaya was that the market had totally collapsed. The millions of rural people who were expected to become new middle-class managers had nothing to manage, and the land was being returned to rice production. As attached as one inevitably becomes to one's ideas in the course of working on them, this was something of a relief. We knew that the actual executors of our plans only half understood them or the rationale behind them. It was too soon. The TV images of American suburbia were too new and too seductive, the infatuation with the car insufficiently tainted by the congestion to come. Maybe, just maybe, another and wiser day of prosperity will come, and someone will pick up these plans like a flag fallen in battle.

Nearness for the Rich: The Case of Adrian Zecha

People who have been in war say that the smell of decomposing flesh is overpoweringly sweet. I have never experienced that smell, nor can I quite imagine it, but it is what comes to mind upon entering the lobby of the Mandarin Hotel on Jalan Thamrin in Jakarta. Clouds of smoke from clove-flavored cigarettes are stirred with the evaporates from bodies entering the frigid lobby from the sweltering outside, mixed with the off-gassed fumes of adhesives and synthetic materials and then recycled ten thousand times through the air conditioning. They don't let much outside air into the system because it is so polluted that on most days the buildings across the street are fuzzy blurs by mid-afternoon. The Mandarin is about fifty stories high as are many of the buildings that bear the names of Western and Japanese corporations along Jalan Thamrin. Behind Jalan Thamrin on both sides stretches a one- and two-story city fabric of ungraspable dimensions that houses 16 million people. In the lobby of the Mandarin, there is a disco, forlorn at all hours, with spots of colored light reflected from the mirror chandelier racing endless laps around the floor. There are usually a couple of Japanese salary men hanging around, looking for one of the mangy prostitutes who wander in occasionally. There is also a "trattoria," which features "Northern Italian Cuisine" that turns the food in your freshman dorm into a fond memory. This is the apogee of "globalizing modernity," Rem Koolhaas's spiritual home.

If you are leaving the Mandarin and your journey is more than a few feet, you have to take a taxi, because at most times of day it is physically impossible to cross Jalan Thamrin on foot. To travel the six blocks to the train station takes close to an hour, an hour spent breathing the fumes of *bajis*, nasty little vehicles powered by two-stroke engines that each emit about as much pollution as a coal-fired electric generating plant.

Imagine that journey, then a numb, sweaty, two-hour train ride to the town of Bandung, then an equally numb and disorienting twilight taxi ride before being deposited in the forecourt of a beautiful new building—a stone-paved court ringed with trees, a thick ochre wall with deep openings and no glass in them. You walk through a passage with no doors and are inside, sort of.

A sublime young lady, demurely wrapped in batik from neck to ankles, hands you a thick iced goblet of delicious fruit juice. There are no living creatures on earth—no fish, no tropical birds, no antelopes, no jungle cats—more graceful and elegant than the young women you see from time to time in Indonesia. On one side of the room, perched on a big pillow, a boy almost as delicate as the fruit juice girl is playing a wooden flute. The flute music mixes with the rustle of trees moving softly in the evening air just outside. On the other side of this semi-outdoor room is a terrace, then a canyon with tall trees reaching from the canyon floor to eye level. Small white birds swirl in the treetops, barely visible in the dim light.

This world and the world of two and a half hours ago cannot both be real. One thinks of the Taoist philosopher Chuang Tzu who could not decide whether he was a man dreaming he was a butterfly, or a butterfly dreaming he was a man. *That* world, the one left behind, is what we are told is inevitable, the product of inexorable technologies and economic forces we cannot control. *This* world, this paradise we have been transported to, is the creation of a Hong Kong entrepreneur named Adrian Zecha.

Zecha and now a few other developers of resorts and hotels in Southeast Asia have discovered the obvious: that the indigenous cultures of Java, Bali, Malaysia, and Thailand include traditions of building, craft, and cuisine that are beautiful and fascinating to travelers from all over the world. Zecha's Chedi Hotel in Bandung, described above, is one of his lesser, middle-priced ventures, yet it is exquisite in every detail—the stoneware jars that hold shampoo, the muslin laundry bag, the little straw trays for tea, the room of lattice screens, the breezy, naturally ventilated building, the gardens, the site itself—all real stuff, all gorgeous, all done without a hint of kitsch. This is not Trader Vic's.

Zecha has a small stable of architects that includes Kerry Hill of Singapore, Ed Tuttle of Paris, and Australian Peter Muller. They are all more or less modern architects; at least they have absorbed and incorporated the lessons of many of the best modernists and the great "premoderns," from Frank Lloyd Wright and Eliel Saarinen (again, not Eero) to Luis Barragan and Rafael Moneo. Their projects include some of the world's most luxurious places, the glorious Amandari and Amanusa Hotels in Bali among them.

So what is the lesson here? One could say that it is the old story of William Morris and the Arts and Crafts movement all over again: Rich people, and rich people only, can afford nice stuff that is made in ways that have integrity and quality. But the interesting story about Adrian Zecha is what he perceives about people's aspirations, what he knows about people's dreams. Certainly not everything about the environments he creates is expensive to produce, and much of their appeal comes from materials and practices that are totally straightforward and simple. But there is something eternal and strangely familiar about these paradisiacal places. We somehow know that they are the way things should be. In them, we feel we have returned to an ancestral home that we have not seen since childhood. They drive home the truth that there is something biological in our responses to places like these and that the lobby of the Jakarta Mandarin Hotel rubs our genetic codes in all the ways they don't want to be rubbed.

CYBERTIME

The automobile and the information revolution are roughly (very roughly) analogous to World War I and World War II. The two great wars were the same conflict with a brief apparent interlude in which fiercer, more devastating technologies were invented along with crazier ideologies and more efficient propaganda.

It is impossible to say, and pointless to speculate, which was the more epic and destructive war. World War I was fought with simple machines, but it changed everything. Automobiles, too, are simple machines, like those of World War I, but these simple, irresistible machines changed cities and buildings forever. The World War I/World War II analogy to the automobile and information technology falls apart when one considers that, for those of us interested in town making, our two wars began at different times, with an interlude between them, but they did not end that way.

We are now waging world wars with the old technology and the new one simultaneously. It is a great shame that architects, planners, and traffic engineers did not master the automobile and its relationship to buildings and townscapes long, long ago, but the fact is we didn't. Because we did not, we now must fight the war with simple technology (the automobile), and the war with the far more complex, and potentially more lethal, information technology at the same time. At least now, far, far too late, we are learning to fight our World War I. It is only now, after decades of catastrophic damage, that we are finally learning to design roads, neighborhoods, blocks, and buildings that accommodate automobiles and town life with reasonable grace. It is still an urgent topic.

The history of the automobile, however, is not just about automobiles. It is a story of industry, public policy, and landscapes. It is about ways of living and ways of making towns and buildings that never existed before: motels, strip malls, power centers, residential planned developments. It is also about a whole range of modes of being, human possibilities that never existed before the automobile—from carhops to Juan Manuel Fangio.

My most cherished bar mitzvah gift was the classic automobile book *Kings of the Road,* by the wondrous writer Ken W. Purdy. As a teenager, I read *Kings of the Road* as many times as a serious student of Islam reads the Koran. My very first time behind the wheel of a car was as a runty fourteen-year-old in my father's fin-tailed '54 Cadillac, stuffed with parents, grandparents, and other relatives. I knew that the heart of the big Cad was a muffled version of the same overhead-valve Kettering V-8 that could send a thundering Cad-Allard from 0 to 100 in twelve seconds flat. I pushed my foot to the floor, and between my grandmother's driveway and the corner, the Cadillac lurched to a thrilling 45 miles per hour, while the assembled relatives went totally berserk.

I used to think that my grandparents had a life experience that was unlike that of any other generation, straddling the transformation from the city of the horse to the postwar automobile suburb and the culture that emanated from it. They grew up in a world that we cannot fully imagine in all of its detail, and they watched that world change day by day into something completely different. It would be so very interesting if they had recorded what was going on, kept a journal of the changes, their impressions, their delight in the new, their sense of loss. As it turns out, their life experience was not unique, and my own generation, for whom the computer will always be newfangled and somewhat alien, is in the midst of a transformation comparable to the one they lived through. We too should keep journals.

Although the computer has not yet inspired an elegy like "She's So Fine, My 409," information technology is similar to the automobile in one important regard: it triggers new modes of being. It is the new human possibilities that accompany the information revolution that so change our lives, our towns, our buildings, the quality of the places we inhabit. The ethos of marketing, media in all its forms, the star system in architecture, and the new culture of management are all curiously intertwined—all the children of the information revolution.

Part 6 considers the world that information technology is making for us, and the strangely entangled web of marketers, managers, stars, star makers, and seekers of stardom that emerge from its influence. All of these people are likely to have an impact on the future of cities as profound as the obsession with automobiles had in the 1950s.

Good Technology, Bad Technology

Amid the interminable, inescapable deluge of punditry that followed the deaths of John F. Kennedy Jr. and Princess Diana, a *Time Magazine* writer contributed the following observation: the intimacy of grief, the deep sense of *personal* loss that millions of people obviously felt at the deaths of JFK Jr. and Princess Diana represents a new inability to distinguish between the virtual world of media experience and the real world of direct experience. He found the stacks of teddy bear offerings creepy.

Architecture and town planning can give some equilibrium to a culture that generates piles of plastic teddy bears as real expressions of virtual grief. They can help people maintain their knowledge of the differences between direct experience and virtual experience and thereby contribute something toward keeping them sane. Air conditioning, the Internet, TV, and voice mail are all OK, all useful, but as a steady unrelenting diet they make you crazy, dull your wits, numb your sensibilities, and make patterns of life in which it becomes harder to distinguish between the death of a loved one and the death of a celebrity.

The ways that architecture and town planning can keep the virtual in check are simple and straightforward:

- Windows that open
- Glass you can see through
- Daylight that is nuanced and related to weather

- Floor plans that don't bury people in the middle of a fluorescent-lit maze that smells of carpet glue
- Places to walk
- Encounters with others, particularly others who are different or not totally predictable
- Real air
- Materials that feel the way they look and are assembled the way they look like they are assembled
- Knowledge of what town you're in and where you are in town
- The sight of farms and wilderness now and then

The windows of our former office gave a beautiful view of downtown San Francisco, the Bay, and the Bay Bridge. We saw big ships go by, and we saw the amazing light conditions when the afternoon fog rolled in and tangled with the skyscrapers of downtown. In our last years there, almost everyone in the office spent hours of each day staring at a computer screen, and we had a problem that we did not have when more of our drawings were done by hand. Most of the people in the office wanted to drop their window blinds all day and shut them tight. They said that even filtered view and light caused eyestrain. In order to be connected to the world through their computers, our workers, like all other office workers, had to disconnect themselves from where they actually were, from the distinctive, memorable place in which they happened to be, from all the nuances of time, weather, and seasons just there on the other side of the miniblind. The cyber world eradicates the phenomenal world. Virtual experience wins; real experience loses.

One important way to assess the benefits of technologies is to consider what they do to the quality of experience. By this measure, air conditioners that disconnect us from the world and vending machines or voice mail that disconnect us from other people are bad technology. Plastic surgery may be good when it restores the features of a burn victim, but bad when it eradicates from a face the record of a lifetime. Bad technology can be useful, even necessary, but it is useful in a bad way. When it comes to "nearness," skis, bicycles, and sailboats are unambiguously good technology, but there is also good in objects that are not so benign, such as fighter planes and race cars. Fighter planes do all sorts of harm, and race cars pollute and burn lots of fossil fuel, but the experience of operating them is utterly thrilling.

Let's consider skis. Certainly they are complex, sly, and technically advanced. Physics, metallurgy, polymer chemistry, and biomechanics all play a part. But the science of the ski means little to the skier who is absorbed with the subtlety of body movement mediating between the force of gravity and the nuances of terrain. The ski is a device to intensify experience. It has similarities, therefore, to a work of art.

No one understands topography better than the cyclist, or tide and wind better than the sailor. For the race car driver, a polar moment of inertia is not just an equation, but a feeling in the hips. The freeway commuter knows nothing of this sensation.

For the phenomenologist—the one for whom consciousness and life itself are wrapped in the data of the senses and the vividness of memory—modernism and its buildings and cities are filled with problems. Surfaces without qualities, light without shadows, rooms in which one loses track of the hour and the season, hills graded flat, heritage erased, universal space in the tropics or the Alps—what has become of us? Through his computer, the secretary of agriculture knows more about the bounty of the earth than the farmer, but unlike the farmer he cannot tell that it is harvest time by the slant of shadows. Why is this true? *Because of his building.* Must this be so? *Let us say no.*

Changes in technology, architecture, and ways of building towns are viewed differently by the economist, the ecologist, and the phenomenologist. The economist worries about money; the ecologist, about the plight of the earth; the phenomenologist, about the quality of human experience. None of them necessarily resists change, but they are all more skeptical about it than the modernist, who views all change as progress.

In the politics of things, however, a potent alliance exists between the modernist's embrace of change and the economist's love of productivity for its own sake. This alliance is so powerful and dangerous that it is politically wise for the ecologist and the phenomenologist to get together and find whatever common ground they have, because they are both so massively threatened by the other coalition. It makes the deepest sense for the phenomenologist, who is completely anthropocentric, and the ecologist, who is not, to join forces. Despite their differences, they do have much in common. We humans evolved in a far more virginal environment than the one we now inhabit, and our appetites are wired accordingly. Strategies to save the planet are frequently similar to those that make the world into a place that feels congenial to us. This is why many in the environmental movement find aboriginal peoples, like Native Americans in their hunter/gatherer state, spiritually appealing.

It would be hard for an eighteenth-century person to imagine that walking, breathing, climbing stairs, seeing people and talking to them, touching things that feel good and knowing what they are, and knowing the time of day and the time of the year could possibly ever be things that would need defending, things whose defense would be the subject of a *movement*, an ideology. Well, there is a lot they couldn't imagine about us, but here we are, adrift in the virtual, hanging on to our humanity in rough seas.

New Words

Perhaps one can learn most about a culture from its neologisms, the words it must invent to describe itself. Consider this list of terms that did not exist fifteen or twenty years ago:

affirmative action officer	*value engineering*	*stakeholders' workshop*
ADA compliance officer	*facilities manager*	*facilitator*
risk management	*information tech*	*expediter*
life cycle cost	*marketing staff*	*formulation document*
peer review engineer	*construction management*	*code consultant*

In the twenty-first century, each of these terms is as familiar to an architect as *metastasize* is to a cancer patient. We all know what those words now mean, and that they carry with them the same foreboding inevitability as *metastasize*. You can struggle and squirm and pray, try medicine and its alternatives—and all or any of those things may work—but the possibility that your tumor will *metastasize* or that your idea will be *value engineered* remains. We live with dread.

Information culture invented the facilities manager to protect itself from another of its great inventions, the visionary genius. There are graduate schools for both where each is carefully taught nothing about the other so that later on in life when they encounter each other it is with that fierce and righteous sense of otherness that Cortez greeted Montezuma. Facilities managers join with construction managers, oversight managers, and other managers in the great act of *value engineering*, a kind of ritual sacrifice, like tearing the hearts from maidens, in which what is most appealing and therefore forbidden is exorcised from the world. It begins as a simple, sensible purgation of waste, but it never ends there. Value engineering in the hands of its adepts rids the physical world of everything that costs a penny more than the most pragmatic service of the immediate short-term task at hand most narrowly defined. What normally does not enter the equation at all, for obvious reasons, is the cost of all the ferocious cost cutters. For most institutions, soft cost (management and a few other things) as a percentage of hard cost (construction) is probably twenty times what it was a few decades ago. It costs *a lot* to make buildings really cheap.

Frank Gehry is the archetype for the kind of visionary genius that feeds the frenzy of facilities managers. Gehry, though a gifted architect by anyone's measure, is a true genius not so much at making buildings but, like his mentor Philip Johnson, at making *news* about buildings. He is a true child of the information age. Greater tectonic wizards of our day—Santiago Calatrava and Michael Hopkins, to name two—are far less celebrated, but stardom has more to do with news than with actual building.

Frank Gehry's charm as a person and as an architect has to do with mischief. He is a mischievous man with mischievous wit, and his buildings are filled with it—mischief with respect to the city and mischief with respect to tectonics, how one builds. Like few others before him, he is the absolute master of the illogical, the great executor of the implausible. The spirit that animates him dominates the culture of architecture schools and is the phenomenon that has led as a reaction to the hegemony of the facilities manager. They think we're all nuts, and they may be only partially wrong.

In the thesis studio of almost every architecture school in the world are rows and rows of young people who want to be Frank Gehry—computer-aided auteurs sculpting autonomous form for the great patrons of the day. Unfortunately, the star system as it exists on earth is different from the star system of the cosmos. Out in the big and ever expanding universe, there is room, apparently, for any number of new stars, galaxies of them, zillions of light years of them. Not so here. There are only so many tenure slots at reputable institutions, only so many museum shows, only so many places for publication. The visionary geniuses who don't fit in these few safe harbors are thrown onto an alien landscape to forage like ice-age wolves, tracked and hunted by facilities managers, trained killers whose mission it is to hack them to bits, to rid the world of them like a pestilence. As the culture of architecture becomes ever more hermetic, solipsistic, and weird, the alternative culture of facilities managers, construction managers, quantity surveyors, and value engineers becomes ever more empowered.

There is a gigantic irony here. The collision of manager culture and genius culture produces a fusion reaction of irresistible force, a spiraling arms race of information technology that, paradoxically, helps produce prosperity and employment as never before. Sixty years ago, the task of designing something, say a college dormitory, involved half a dozen people and took a couple of months. Now there are hundreds, indirectly thousands, involved, and it takes twenty times, fifty times longer. The dormitory itself is not nearly so nice to live in or look at, and it won't last nearly as long as the old one, but nobody really notices or cares.

What's more, each one of the hundreds of people involved in the simplest act of building has an expensive computer that will be junked after a year or two and software that needs upgrading every few months, usually requiring each of the hundreds of people to take new software lessons. All of the managers, affirmative action officers, code consultants, and all the rest are linked in cyberspace, endlessly revising what one another does, all armed to the teeth with short-lived software and hardware that is obsolete before it stops smelling new. That is the secret to our economy, our prosperity, our well-being. High-tech drives the economy; the big list of neologisms drives high-tech.

Ninety percent of the work of our office is created by the prosperity of Silicon Valley. Without high-tech there would be no housing to design, no San Francisco lofts, no dormitories at Stanford, no redevelopment blocks in San Jose. The American economy at the beginning of this millennium is successful and thriving not because of the quantity or quality of its production, but because of its fabulous, stupefying inefficiency—the army of people and, more important, products it takes to *do* anything.

This titanic struggle between manager culture and genius culture has many casualties. In a war, both sides keep track of their dead and wounded: the fallen geniuses, the not quite geniuses, and the facilities managers whose projects go over budget. In this great war, however, it is the *collateral damage* that is more interesting and more tragic than the official casualty list. Collateral damage in this case includes much of the physical world, the scarred and polluted battlefield on which the war is waged. The Thousand-Year Reich came and went in twelve horrific years. The damage was beyond measure, but it did end. Perhaps the Fourth Reich of the facilities managers will end too, even though it is now impossible to see when or why.

The Interview

This was it, the big time—short-listed as design lead in a joint venture with big corporate firms, competing with national heavyweights for a complicated $80 million university project. The first meeting of the joint venture was a video conference (my first) to begin our preparation for The Interview. The video conference place was in a downtown high-rise near my office—lots of little rooms with attractive *done-up* young women scurrying in and out. It looked like a brothel for which you would make an Internet reservation and pay with a credit card, if there is such a thing, or maybe a fancy place to get a root canal. I don't know what the video conference accomplished that a phone call would not have, but it took a long time to arrange and cost $275 for ten minutes. We decided about my flight arrangements to meet for the *real* preparation for The Interview and what I would bring with me.

I got there mid-afternoon on Interview eve. I was shown into a conference room sized for a Chinese wedding banquet, with half a dozen little knots of people in the midst of furious preparations. There was a big stack of dirty dishes in the corner, and some people were still munching on pizza as they worked. Everyone seemed so totally preoccupied that I began to chat with the young woman I found myself next to, who said she worked for the architect who was my host. I asked her what she did, and she replied "market segment tri-folds." She said she was a communications major and worked in the marketing department. She handed me two folded pieces of stiff paper twenty-five inches by eleven inches. One was titled "Education" and the other "Entertainment Retail." My God, what *were* these things? Every color in the rainbow, computer image superimposed on computer image. Flashier, glitzier than a duty-free catalog, more like "Coming This Summer to Marine World." The two pieces of paper were more or less identical, but the buildings they showed were every which way—some modern, some revivalist sort of, some more vernacular sort of, most not so bad, some not not so bad.

Then the senior partners of the two corporate firms came into the room. It was snowing out, and they both had on overcoats and really nice hats. Handsome men, full of oomph. Everyone gathered around the heliport-sized conference table.

Our host laid out the strategy for The Interview. The project had been funded two years ago with a three-and-a-half-year fixed schedule. Eighteen months to go, and the managers were just now ready to select the architect. They were in a big panic, and most of the interview panel had their jobs on the line. Schedule was key. On-time delivery. I didn't get it. Eighteen months? Eighty million dollars? Complicated program, public process, "stakeholders." No frigging way.

Our host had a strategy—*"a modified semi-design build-fast-track-guaranteed-maximum-price-negotiated-contact"*—except you couldn't quite call it any of those things because of university prohibitions on exactly those ways of doing business. In other words, find a contractor who would start building something next week for a fixed price, and everyone would worry about what he was building as he went along. The idea was to get all the managers to agree to call this process something else to save their own skins. Our host also had the contractor, the fixed price, and the contractor's schedule to present at The Interview. That's what all the pizza munchers were working on. What a concept!

Then came the dress rehearsal. The marketing staff (about six people) played the interview panel. I did the first five minutes on building design, and the other guest principal did five minutes on urban design. Then came thirty minutes of spiel about schedule and process with lots of charts and spreadsheets. Our host would talk about our software compatibility with the university system and our "existing fully operational video conference capability." The whole interview, including questions, had to fit in one hour because there were seven teams competing. It is hard even to guess how many hundreds of thousands of dollars of time and effort that represented.

The design part was squished into ten minutes because there were no planners or design architects on the panel, just the managers of various kinds and one woman from the Housing Office, a "stakeholder." Odd because the university had just paid handsomely for a bold, brilliant master plan by Toronto urban designer Ken Greenberg. The "Formulation Document" prepared by the managers and one of the competing architects was obviously done by people who neither understood nor gave a damn about Greenberg's beautiful master plan.

The last part of the dress rehearsal consisted of the marketing staff grilling the architects and contractors' project managers with all kinds of tough, esoteric questions about procedures. Lots of people kibitzed about what the answers should be, and there was a designated answerer for every conceivable question. It took hours. Late to bed, then up early to get the whole clatter of easels, projectors, charts, and stuff to The Interview site.

The Interview was just like the dress rehearsal except for two things. First, my co–guest principal sprouted a persona for The Interview that was quite unlike his gracious but low-key demeanor of the day before. He became an absolute charmer, passionate, articulate, and like he was fresh from the charismatician, as they say in Washington. He obviously loved this sort of thing. Second, the questions from the managers were all puffballs. All that rehearsal for not much.

After The Interview, we had a little warm down at the office, and then I went to lunch with my two co-venturers. Mostly I listened. Mostly they shared information about their marketing programs: $1.5 million and $1.1 million a year, respectively. They were both concerned about marketing cost containment and how important timesheet design was. One said that, to hold costs down, his office was still using Powerpoint. *Still using Powerpoint.* I had seen a Powerpoint slide show for the first time a couple of weeks before. To me, it was a brand-new technology—slick, but many times more elaborate, cumbersome, and expensive than the old way of showing images. To my hosts, it was old, cheap, and simple.

Then we went to the airport. My co–guest principal was off to another interview, his third of the week, and I had the long ride home to think about all that I had learned in twenty-five hours about architectural practice in the Information Age. As I dozed on the plane, the phrase *"still using Powerpoint"* kept ringing in my head. What was next, after Powerpoint? Promotional videos, perhaps. Maybe with original musical scores. Would it be next year or the year after that the Marketing Department would include a film crew? Maybe there would be a couple of in-house composers. Then there would be sound editors and mixers. Pretty soon every architectural firm would have its own little *Cinecittà*, where the architecture and planning has the status of props or art direction. Then, of course, it could all be simulated digitally, and there would be no need for reality at all. Airplane sleep can be fitful.

We didn't get the job.

SIGNS OF LIFE

It is easy enough for a student of the world to fill the entire sketchbook of his travels with gloomy pictures. This pessimistic student can imagine spending all of his days in endless preparation for The Interview, flying from place to place without ever leaving the same ubiquitous and featureless no-place. He imagines that there must once have been a time when the obstacles to simple pleasures were smaller and fewer, when it was easier to build things that were gratifying to make and to use, and when it was cheaper to buy good peaches He likes cars, but he sees a world overrun with them, with more roads and more sprawl, and his heart quivers. But his dark sketchbook—though it is full of detailed and accurate recordings of things—does not convey some of the most important goings-on, unless you look at it very closely and know how to look.

The painter Mark Rothko was a special kind of genius, and he demanded from those who look at his work, especially the large paintings that he did near the end of his life, participation in his way of seeing. You cannot look at a late Rothko and see what is really there without entering his spirit. His last canvases are completely black; those just earlier are monumental shapes of dark purples or reds on backgrounds that are almost the same color. At a first glance or a second one, they are strong and simple, even simplistic. But if you put yourself in front of a late Rothko and stay there for a while, you may enter into a meditation with the painting, and it will reveal a universe to you. Not immediately, but after a time, the black surfaces or the purple ones become a hundred different blacks or purples, shimmering in what is no longer a two-dimensional surface but has become the deepest mathematical space, beyond our normal experience. Who knows what demons Rothko found in those depths, or just why he took his own life, but his canvases show us is that if one looks properly, darkness and flatness are full of energies and portents, complexities and shafts of light that dazzle in their dimness. He provides us with a better way of looking at the dark sketchbook of the student of the world, one that can lead from nihilism to hope to action—that is, if you look at it for a long time and in the right way.

Part 7 chronicles the efforts of small groups of people who have stared into the darkness and found shafts of light.

CNU

People interested in cities should think about orthopedists. Many other doctors think of orthopedists the way that carpenters think of sheetrockers, as somewhat brutish, one-dimensional characters in a crude but necessary subdiscipline. Like any other stereotype, this one is blatantly unfair, because there must be orthopedists who don't think like orthopedists, just as there are traffic engineers who don't think like traffic engineers, and disability advocates who have more in their heads than wheelchairs. But just think about the stereotype and how it came into being.

Who hasn't had an experience something like the following: You have a pain, a pain in the butt so pervasive and annoying that it's hard to think about anything else. It's not there every minute, but every time you move a certain way—YAAAUGH—there it is, and it's taken over your life. So you go to an orthopedist, who orders a $1,500 MRI. When the result comes back, the orthopedist is all smiles and he says, "Good news, there is nothing really wrong with you. No neuroskeletal abnormalities or damage whatsoever. It's just soft tissue stuff. Here's a prescription for codeine."

The fact that codeine is addictive and can cause brain damage is not an issue. And neuromuscular pains as opposed to neuroskeletal pains are not only in another specialty, they are the subject of osteopathy—another degree. Osteopaths are not even in the AMA. So you don't have a problem, at least not a real, treatable orthopedic problem. So go try your brain on codeine and let your muscles atrophy from nerve damage, or try alternative treatment if you want to (insurance now covers some of it), but there is nothing really wrong with you.

The orthopedist—the curriculum he was trained within, the whole administrative apparatus of medical schools and of research funding, the organization of hospitals—is the product of a certain model of the human organism. It is a nineteenth-century model that breaks the body into discrete systems: the gastrointestinal system, the musculoskeletal system, the nervous system (which even nineteenth-century medicine conceded had some connection to the mind), and so on.

This nineteenth-century model of the body as discrete systems is, in fact, the structure of the medical establishment. In every medical school in the world, each of these supposedly discrete systems is represented by a tenured faculty, a research budget, a space allocation, a set of journals, peer review, the whole entrenched, institutional schmegegy that people build their careers upon.

The recent great breakthroughs in medical science, the pathbreaking stuff of Nobel Laureates, are realizations that the discrete systems of the nineteenth-century century curriculum actually interact with one another, and that, in fact, the model itself may be a meaningless or deceptive way to describe an organism as complex as a human. So much of the leading edge of biomedical research now crosses the boundaries of the old specialties that some medical schools now offer budget incentives to their faculties to disband their old departmental structures and participate in research and practice that according to the old model is "interdisciplinary."

The analogy to cities is obvious. The ravages of segregated land use (houses here, apartments there, commerce someplace else, culture in the cultural center), the dissociation of transportation from city building, of buildings from streets, of public policy from design, are the city's equivalent of the visit to the orthopedist. Le Corbusier loved the singleminded rationalism of American highways as he discovered them in 1935, but he despised the complexity of the traditional urban street. We have learned, painfully, how misguided his affections were. The American traffic engineer, circa 1935 to 1995, was the mutant child of the Enlightenment—like the orthopedist, a *reductio ad absurdum* of the classification of knowledge. The Congress for the New Urbanism was conceived in a shared moment of pure hubris as an attempt to rescue American cities from the twin scourges of untreated chronic back pain and codeine addiction.

In 1992, six of us, all friends and professional colleagues, decided that it was time to act out a fantasy we had discussed now and then for a long time. We all believed that the work we were each doing as architects, planners, and teachers was similar in spirit to that of the others, and also to lots of other people's work, not only in planning and architecture but also in other disciplines (according to *our* old model of what constitutes a discipline). Though we each were operating independently, we sensed that we were part of what was at least a latent movement. The subject of this movement was a reaction to the calamity of suburban sprawl in the United States—its devastation of both the landscape and the historic fabric of older cities, the dismal quality of life it promoted, and its stupefying ugliness. Our views were rooted not only in our own work but in the writing and teaching of several people whom we all admired— Jane Jacobs, Colin Rowe, and Leon Krier among them.

According to our fantasy, we would convene a great meeting and invite everyone we could think of who was doing similar work or had similar views, not only in our own fields but in related fields, that could be helpful to us. As we planned the meeting, the idea expanded to a series of four meetings, each devoted to aspects of the subject. At the end of the four meetings, the conference proceedings could be edited into a book that would present a vision of an alternative to the way man-made habitat in the United States was being constructed. In our more grandiose moments, we dreamt of a book that might have the impact that *The Athens Charter* had had for an earlier generation.

After a protracted wrangle among us about what to call these events, we settled on the name Congress for the New Urbanism (CNU). The first Congress was convened in Alexandria, Virginia, in 1993 with two hundred invitees, many of them the most distinguished people we could name in architecture, planning, and public policy along with academics, politicians, and developers. To our astonishment, virtually all of the two hundred invitees showed up in Alexandria.

Since then, the CNU has become something more and something different from anything we imagined. As this is written, it has 2,500 members and is growing steadily. It has an executive director, a full-time staff of seven, task forces, committees, a board of directors, and the whole apparatus of a major advocacy organization. We realized that we had launched something that had gone far beyond our expectations in an unforgettable moment at the fourth Congress in 1996 in the beautiful Dock Street Theater in Charleston, South Carolina. In the days preceding the Congress, a great flurry of faxes, e-mails, and long meetings had produced the final wording of the Charter for the New Urbanism. Henry Cisneros, the charismatic and visionary secretary of housing and urban development, came to Charleston to sign the Charter. In an electrifying speech, Cisneros declared that the Charter would now become the statement of policy for HUD during his tenure and would guide his agency in its efforts to tear down and replace the worst of the nation's public housing.

At that moment, we had the dizzying sensation of suddenly being players, not just commentators, not just teachers, not just isolated practitioners or consultants with our inconsequential little opinions about things, but real players in a real ball game in a real stadium with a real crowd. It is not as if individually or collectively we have all leaped from triumph to triumph since that thrilling day, but neither have things ever been quite the same as they were before. For all of us, the stakes are higher, the sense of purpose is more clear, the rewards are more tangible, and what we do has more meaning for others. The sense of being part of something that is collective and at least partially successful is an amazing narcotic.

HUD is not the only dragon that has breathed the ether of New Urbanism in the last several years. The Urban Land Institute (ULI) is a large, powerful developer's organization that for decades had a relationship to traditional cities and urban structure that was not unlike the National Rifle Association's relationship to gun control. Aspiring developers joined the ULI and paid handsomely for its conferences and seminars to learn exactly how to make money by building suburban sprawl. There are ULI pamphlets and how-to books on every element of the landscape of sprawl—business parks, shopping centers of all sorts, gated golf course subdivisions, everything one encounters on the road outside Dallas or Phoenix or almost any part of America built since 1965.

But suddenly, in the last couple of years, the ULI's policy statements and propaganda have begun to sound curiously like the Charter for the New Urbanism, spouting such notions as walkable neighborhoods, mixed use, and even (shockingly) the virtues of places where people of different incomes might come in contact with one another. Somehow, someone or some group of influential people has had an epiphany.

To see the impact of New Urbanist thinking on mainstream development practice, one should take a tour of recently built projects in Silicon Valley, as I did with a group of planners and developers in the summer of 2002. The tour covered much of the same ground as a similar tour in 1985, when we were beginning a long, complicated consulting job to the San Jose Department of City Planning, writing the San Jose Housing Design Guidelines. The 1985 tour visited thirty-seven new planned developments, and I remember it as a descent into hell. It hard to say which was worse—the worlds inside the PDs or the "town" they made in aggregation. If Heidegger had written about these projects, he would have called his essay "Dwelling, Parking and Parking." After thirty-seven hideous PDs, my mind spun in a delirium of parking drives, garage doors, sound walls, and almost nothing else. The only human being we encoun tered in the thirty-seven projects was one forlorn lady, jogging laps around a parking lot.

The 2002 tour was very different. The overriding impression after a whole day of visiting new projects in the communities of Silicon Valley—San Jose, Mountain View, Milpitas, Palo Alto—is that of the Charter of the New Urbanism lurking behind an unevenly murky sheet of glass. It is far from a perfect world, but there clearly are developers and architects who really understand and support at least some of the principles of the Charter, and most are either trying to or are being forced to in order to receive their entitlements.

Some of the new PDs actually connect more or less seamlessly to others in something resembling the fabric of a town, and the handling of parking has been completely transformed. Townhouses have their garages behind them, and single houses have either alleys or side drives, like Craftsman bungalows. There are no more new streets lined with garage doors, or parking drives that constitute the public realm. Streets have entries, porches, trees and, from time to time, people on them. The downtowns of Mountain View, Palo Alto, and San Jose are also completely transformed from sad, derelict places into thriving little urban centers, with good restaurants and life on the streets.

In all of this, one clearly sees the hands of certain key people, some with Berkeley urban design training and most of them members of CNU: Leslie Gould as Mountain View planning director, Michael Friedman as urban design consultant to Mountain View, Tom Aidala as urban design director for the San Jose Redevelopment Agency, Gary Schoenauer as San Jose planning director, Peter Calthorpe as architect and planner for the Crossings in Mountain View, and many others, to be sure.

If the CNU has had an impact far beyond its founders' expectations, it is because it is a peculiar mix of people and ways of thinking. All of the founders of the CNU are architects, all restless within the normal confines of the subject. The topic of the CNU is the American metropolis as it is viewed not only or principally by architects but by all sorts of people—politicians, developers, bureaucrats, social workers, transportation planners. The CNU is now nothing less than a practical working model of a theory of knowledge that can save us all from the ravages of specialization, the hyperclassification of knowledge, and the monocultures of single issues.

The diverse membership of the CNU shifts the focus of architects and planners, who value the city, from the cultural battleground on relativistic quicksand that dominates the academy and the professional press, to the terra firma of a political, environmental, and social battle in which we have many allies and many weapons. For some of us, it has also changed the nature of our work and changed our own perceptions about it. Experience within the CNU has so enlarged our own abilities to conceptualize what it is we are doing that the work itself appeals to a constituency a hundred times broader and more powerful than any that our work addressed ten years ago. Our own orthopedic tendencies have not survived our long, intense encounter with one another.

HOPE VI

One of the defining characteristics of a Jewish mother, which I had in spades, was to ascribe earth-shaking importance to whatever her-son-the-architect was doing. On her deathbed in 1996, she insisted on knowing, as she always did, what I was up to. I told her that I had been invited the following week to Harvard to help present the principles of the Charter for the New Urbanism to HUD and Housing Authority officials at the request of HUD secretary Henry Cisneros. Cisneros organized this conference shortly after signing the charter in Charleston. She knew all about the principles of the charter, had in fact offered some unsolicited edits when we were writing them, and knew about the ambitions of Secretary Cisneros (whom she admired greatly) with respect to public housing. I told her that, given her condition, there was no way that I would go. After all, it was just another conference—no big deal, my buddies would do fine, and I wouldn't be missed.

On her deathbed, she was full of admonitions and instructions that insured that she would be firmly in charge of all sorts of things long after she was gone. The Israeli novelist Amos Oz has said that, when it comes to directing the lives of her sons, no Jewish mother has ever let her own death stand in the way. From me she extracted a promise that no matter what, no matter when she died or when the funeral was, I would not miss the Harvard/HUD conference. It was, she said, "the most important thing you have ever had the chance to do." True to her character, she willed the timing of her death and her funeral so that I did not have a conflict.

The HUD/CNU event at Harvard in 1996 turned out to be a memorably tough, confrontational event. The Congress for the New Urbanism was asked by Secretary Cisneros to discuss public housing from our own point of view. We all felt that the history of public housing in the United States was a desperately sad tale. What began in the Catherine Bauer era as the most high-minded New Deal activism was transformed into a horror story that had stigmatized, isolated, and trapped the poor and had left deep wounds in American cities. Some unknowable combination of modern movement hubris, bureaucratic clumsiness, and congressional stinginess had made a big dose of poison, and one had only to drive around almost any American city to see the scars it left.

From Roosevelt's signing of the Public Housing Act of 1937, in which Catherine Bauer figured so prominently, until that momentous Saturday morning in 1996 when the HUD limousine, fender flags all a-flutter, pulled up to the Dock Street Theater in Charleston—America's basic policy toward housing its poorest citizens was clear and unswerving. Public housing should serve people temporarily; no one should be stuck in it for long. And whether the nation and the Congress was in the mood to build lots of public housing, or barely to maintain what existed, the relationship of housing to money was the same: the largest number of units for the fewest dollars, no matter what.

Since 1937, public housing administrators had shared a vision with the architects who served them. They had an overarching belief in their own good sense and a reciprocal contempt for the messy, grimy, irrational legacy of the American city. By simply clearing bits of it away, it was possible to build rationally and make a few dollars serve many. The utter hell on earth that this vision produced now needs no description. Those squalid, soul-destroying crack havens are seared into the national memory and the national conscience as a collective blunder with few rivals— slavery, Viet Nam, maybe Prohibition for stupidity, if not perniciousness. The list is short.

Many of us who had designed low-income housing believed that there were alternatives to what public housing typically had been. We had all worked for nonprofits whose existence depended on providing low-income housing by stealth. If their projects were not indistinguishable from the neighborhoods they were part of, they simply didn't get built.

But here we were talking to career federal bureaucrats, and we were keenly aware that much of our audience felt that their lifework was being assaulted by what we had to say. In 1996, many of them still wrapped themselves in the cape of the New Deal, and they saw the same antipoor agenda in what we were saying that they saw in welfare reform. In their own eyes, they, and they alone, constituted the last safety net for the poor in an increasingly indifferent society. They, at least the most vocal ones, defended what seemed to us the indefensible. For most of us, changing the direction of HUD and Housing Authorities appeared to be a hopeless undertaking. It seemed that we were trying to move a vast mountain with our tiny beach shovels, and we left feeling that we had not contributed anything that would make the slightest difference.

Somehow, by some miraculous alchemy, something quite amazing happened after that conference at Harvard. It is a piece of history that someone who knows the ins and outs of HUD in the Clinton years should write, because it represents a watershed in American urban policy. The names of a few of the leading actors in the story are Secretary Henry Cisneros, Cisneros's deputy Marc Weiss, Secretary Andrew Cuomo, most importantly deputy undersecretary Elinor Bacon, Milan Ozdinec of HUD, and Ray Gindroz of the Congress for the New Urbanism. Obviously, there were many others.

I knew that what they accomplished was miraculous by the time of my next participation in a HUD conference at Baltimore in 1999. In the short interval of three years, the New Urbanist principles that were introduced at Harvard had become embedded as a real part of the culture of HUD. HUD had embarked on HOPE VI, a vast program to tear down the worst public housing in the country, much of which was uninhabitable or nearly so, and build in its place new neighborhoods where public housing was mixed with partially subsidized and nonsubsidized market rate houses. The intent was to blend the public housing population seamlessly into the fabric of towns, partially by reviving local traditions of architecture and urbanism and partially by implementing ambitious programs of job training and education. An explicit statement of New Urbanist principles was included in the funding criteria for HOPE VI grants to housing authorities.

At Baltimore we told the story again, this time to an audience dominated by a spirit totally different from that of 1996. We reviewed the New Urbanist perspective on where federal efforts at city building had gone awry, and we amplified upon New Urbanist design principles as they had been edited and tailored to the needs of HOPE VI.

Then we looked critically at works in progress, but there was hardly a need for us to serve as critics, because a large part of the audience could evaluate what was shown as well as we could and with as much conviction. Not everything we saw was good work; maybe half was and half wasn't. But it was not just we, the so-called faculty, who reacted to the badly designed projects. Other architects, HUD officials, lots of Housing Authority people, and a highly articulate contingent of public housing tenants jumped all over those presenters who showed poorly designed streets, or segregated the public housing tenants, or didn't connect gracefully to the neighborhoods around their projects.

For all the effort Bill Clinton has made to shine a glowing light of history on his presidency, he has made no claims as a builder. In this regard, he is not a Francois Mitterand or a Tony Blair, let alone a Franklin Roosevelt. But the Clinton administration's one achievement in city design and urban policy is enormous; that is, what Clinton's HUD achieved through HOPE VI. It reversed the direction of fifty years of federal policies responsible for the era in which the poor of the nation were segregated, identified, and warehoused in the squalor of public housing projects. The bad trip that started with so much ingenuous zeal under Franklin Roosevelt finally was brought to a close starting in May 1994.

Cisneros's signature of the Charter for the New Urbanism proved to be no empty gesture, because it marked a fundamental shift in the course of social housing in the United States for the first time in forty-five years. What the Charter of the New Urbanism declares, among other things, is that the building or maintaining of segregated enclaves of the poor is a bad, bad idea. The poor should not be identified and trapped by the houses they live in. By the year 2000, HUD demolished 103,000 units of its worst hovels and replaced most (not all) with new houses that declare that the American city was not so dumb in the first place, that people's affections for their neighborhoods were not misplaced.

At this writing, HOPE VI continues after a fashion in the Bush administration and is like some psychopharmacological wonder pill that returns a mad uncle to sanity after he has spent fifty years crazy as a loon. We and many other architects are helping HUD and HUD-funded Housing Authorities (of all people) to build sensible, straightforward, sometimes even beautiful neighborhoods, the kind that used to be the basic fabric of American cities. Different sorts of people—renters and homeowners, working-class people, poor people, and middle-class people—live together on nice streets with trees and porches. Cars move slowly. There are backyards and privacy, neighborliness, pride of ownership, safety, and security, and you can walk to the store or your kid can.

The most curious thing about Clinton's grand urban achievement is that he has never given a single indication that he noticed its occurrence. Not once during Al Gore's stumbling run for the presidency was it mentioned. When HOPE VI received the coveted Innovation in American Government Award as the outstanding program in government in the year 2000 (beating 2,500 other federal programs), Clinton didn't say a word. When he delivered the benediction to his own presidency, crediting himself for everything good that happened during eight years of the events of the world, he talked about almost everything conceivable, but not HOPE VI. Does he really know what happened, how momentous it was, what a shift of history he presided over? Is he proud of these events or disappointed that no more occurred? Does he give a damn? Did that $3 billion just sneak by surreptitiously? Are you really sneaks, Secretary Andrew Cuomo, Deputy Undersecretary Elinor Bacon, and your pals or did he know what you were up to? How will we ever know?

The HOPE VI achievement extends beyond the public housing it has replaced. Though critics can point to flaws in the program or many projects that are executed less well than the best ones, HOPE VI has helped in a clear, tangible way to reestablish America's skills at city building. What is most astonishing to those of us who participated in those difficult few days at Harvard in 1996 is that it is HUD and Housing Authorities (not all, but more than a few) that have led the way. As I have had to admit grudgingly often in my life, my mother had it right.

Monuments

The simpleminded observation that cities consist of a few monuments and a fabric of buildings in which most people live and work is true enough to latch a theory upon. This book focuses on that idea, and particularly on the making of city fabric as opposed to monuments, for a couple of reasons. First, partially by choice and partially by happenstance, the building of city fabric has been the focus of my lifework. The nagging question remains, whether for an architect this is a make-do, second-rate destiny or a desperately needed grappling with a tragically neglected topic. Undoubtedly, it is some of both.

The absence of a theory of city fabric has been damaging cities for a long time, but worse has been the common perception among architects and teachers of the subject that *fabric,* the great majority of the built world, is a second-rate issue, one not worthy of attention or aspiration. Kenneth Frampton's dismissive description of normative building as a "banal, almost metabolic activity" epitomizes an attitude that creates a big problem. For the hippest professors of architecture, the word "normative" is a term of ridicule or revulsion, reserved for the work of students who just don't get it. I shall never forget the booming contralto of deconstructivist star Zaha Hadid ricocheting off a terrified third-year student at Columbia (Frampton's school): "IT LOOKS LIKE A GODDAMN BUILDING!" Imagine daring to show a drawing of a building that looked like a building to Zaha Hadid.

It is a tragedy for the world, and for the many people who

compete fiercely with one another for chances to make some of the world, that most of them do not aspire to make most of the world. One cannot teach in a school of architecture for decades, touching the lives of thousands of students, and not be overcome with sadness at the poignant nuttiness of this situation. So many of those earnest, striving students have nothing but disappointment to face. So many of them could also contribute so much and receive gratification from it if only they thought about the making of town fabric a little differently.

To help build that different way of thinking, the preceding essays have focused on the largely neglected topic of normative city building, with all of its insanely complex constraints of budgets, codes, marketing pressures, and the rest. But this argument about fabric and monument would be incomplete if it did not consider the part of the equation that has for the most part *not* been the focus of my own work but is the focus of almost every other architect's dreams: the making of monuments, unconstrained by all those terrible forces represented in the Tribunal of the Grand Inquisitors. To tell the truth, I too dream of making monuments— it's just that I don't do it every night, and I will not feel that my life has gone too badly if I never get another chance to build one.

Some architects undoubtedly are better monument makers than others, and some build in ways that serve the cities of which their monuments are part better than others. Like other branches of the entertainment industry, the architectural profession has its share of shallow celebrities, whose principal claim to fame is fame itself. One of the things that the shallowness of the shallow consists of is the confusion of fabric with monument. The world we live in would be a noticeably nicer place if this confusion never existed and if there were no attention-seeking architects, grasping at big opportunities through the notoriety generated by the eccentric treatment of normative buildings.

The relationship of fame to architectural careers is insidious. It turns even sensible, talented architects into troubadours who trot around the world upon demand, performing their own repertoire of personological stylistics, sometimes consisting of one tune, sung over and over, whatever the setting, whoever the patron, and whatever the group of users they are ostensibly serving. But the star system is too deeply embedded in media-driven culture to think that things could be very different. Monuments are designed by stars, and all architects want to be stars. That leaves the question—which is the brightest star? Who is the best living architect, and how does one make such a determination?

In some ways this is a fatuous question, like "Who is the most beautiful woman in the world?" Marion Jones is without question the *fastest* woman in the world—10.65 seconds for 100 meters—no question about it. But *the most beautiful*? That's different. There are many candidates, and many kinds of candidates, for the most-beautiful-woman-in-the-world. But how do you compare a Balinese teenager to a Swedish aristocrat or a black sprinter? The title best-living-architect also has many candidates, and they are best in different ways. Kenneth Frampton has long championed the Portuguese architect Alvaro Siza. Spain's Rafael Moneo was a favorite of Colin Rowe. My own short list of candidates would include Renzo Piano, who has traveled a fascinating path since his bombastic debut on the world scene at the Centre Pompidou with Richard Rogers in 1977. His recent work has reached amazing heights of poetic inventiveness based on environmental concerns—the qualities of light and air, energy use, and so on. For sheer spectacle, technical wizardry, and flawless execution, it is hard for anyone to compete with Santiago Calatrava, whose fantastic buildings actually open and close, walk around, and flap their wings.

According to the criteria of locating people in time and space, gratifying their sensory appetites, and creating buildings that reinforce the unique qualities of places, there is one architect who is operating with more depth and intelligence than anyone else. He is also not so very famous. Michael Hopkins is the inverse of a media star. He probably doesn't even *own* an unstructured black jacket. He has taken the time to publish two beautiful monographs of the work of his firm, but nothing else. No *New Yorker* profiles, never a picture in *W*, no Charlie Rose interviews, nothing like that. If Charlie Rose were to spend ten minutes with this soft-spoken, grandfatherly man, he would decide correctly that he would make lousy television.

In fact, Hopkins is an architect of stunning range and accomplishment who is simply too busy with architecture and a rich family life to bother courting fame. His career has not depended upon the relentless treadmill of self-promotion that for most architects is a survival mechanism they cannot live without. All of Hopkins's work to date has been in

England, except for one project in Scotland, and most architects outside the United Kingdom, even those who read professional journals every month, have never heard of him. For reasons I do not fully understand, his life circumstance has not demanded that he publish all over the world and then frantically run around, doing a Hop-Hopkins here and a Hop-Hopkins there, as is the fate of most others of his stature.

Hopkins has devoted his attentions to the evolution of a method of practicing architecture that is far beyond the outdated dogmas and bromides of modernism but does not slide back into a nostalgic historicism. His work is based on important issues that are both current and timeless. He and his colleagues are relentlessly inventive, without feeling the need constantly to flog us with their cleverness or personal genius. The works deal with clearly formulated topics—environment, tectonics, utility, and urbanism—but they are not dry treatises on these subjects. The buildings are extraordinarily beautiful.

Some clearly point to the roots of Hopkins's career in the office of that master of high-tech Norman Foster. When the occasion demands, Hopkins and his team can produce the most exquisitely engineered and machined artifacts of stainless steel, titanium, or precast concrete. But unlike Foster, when Hopkins builds a laboratory in a medieval village in Dorsetshire, he is perfectly willing to make it out of load-bearing rubble masonry in the normal and ancient way and to give the building a pitched slate roof. There is no scenographic historicism here, just straightforward mastery of the materials and crafts that are indigenous to the place and that locate his building in the legacy of the town. His simple, uncontrived, and timeless way of building helps the town itself to be a living thing, not a fossilized relic.

His interest in, and mastery of, techniques and materials is completely unconstrained by ideological prescriptions and proscriptions about *our time* or any other time. He is neither a Zeitgeister nor a revivalist. He can build skillfully in wood, in orlon fabric, in steel, bronze, or aluminum, in masonry or concrete. Hopkins's tectonics, the expressive way that his buildings deal with material and technique, owes much to his study and admiration of Louis Kahn, particularly Kahn's masterful Exeter Library (1965–72). Kahn was a builder/technician par excellence, and he was the first major architect of the postwar years to slide out from under modernism's dogma about time. Kahn mastered both modern building techniques and ancient ones. He was as fluent and inventive in brick as he was in precast concrete. His buildings, and perhaps the Exeter Library most eloquently, have a quality of timelessness. The bricks at Exeter make one think not of newness but of continuity, of our bond across time with the people who fired the kilns and laid the walls and arches for Marcellus Agrippa, architect of the Pantheon.

Hopkins learned from Kahn, incorporated Kahn, and moved into realms of urbanism, landscape, and environmentalism that Kahn never considered. Kahn turned construction into a timeless poetic of haunting beauty. Hopkins does the same for a whole range of subjects. Hopkins, blessedly, has never caught onto the fashionable idea of the *liberation* of architecture into some realm of the mind beyond the constraints of context, environment, technique, program, and history. The poetry of his architecture is the sum of those things, and it is nothing else.

To an extraordinary degree, Hopkins's work embodies two opposite, contradictory traits. First, there is a slow evolution of the same ideas, techniques, and details from project to project. The flat brick arches, from Rome via Kahn, that made their first appearance in a Hopkins building at the Glyndebourne Opera House (1989–94) are repeated in variation at the Queens Building, Emmanuel College (1993–95) and the Sheltered Housing, Charterhouse (1994–2000). Glyndebourne Opera House also began his investigation of the expressive possibilities of combining tapering brick piers with highly refined precast concrete beams that penetrate through the supporting piers and rhythmically punctuate their outer surface. At his Inland Revenue Center (1992–95), the penetrating beam evolves with stunning originality into a gracefully curved shallow vault that performs a variety of roles structurally, environmentally, and aesthetically. The vaults span all the way across the building and serve as both the finished ceiling and the actual fireproof structural subfloor. The undulating vaults penetrate the facade and rest on exquisitely crafted precast imposts that interrupt load-bearing prefabricated brick piers at each floor. On the facade, beneath each vault is a delicate, fritted glass "light-shelf" that reflects daylight onto the vault, deep into the plan. Never before in a modern building, not even in the best of Kahn, have issues of structure, construction, environment, and utility found such expressive and brilliantly congruent resolution. Hopkins revisited this set of elements again for his masterpiece to date, the New Parliamentary Building, completed in 2000.

At the same time as this patient evolution of repeated ideas is going on, each project is uniquely directed at its particularities of context. He is a contextualist, but not a slavish one, and he uses a whole variety of strategies to respond to the places of which his buildings are a part. The rubble-masonry, pitched roof Pilkington Laboratories at the Sherborne School, Dorsetshire (1995–2000) are one version of a Hopkins building that reinforces the special qualities of a place by translating a modern program and building methods into structures that are not very different from ancient ones nearby. Conversely, for the "Dynamic Earth" complex at Salisbury Crags in Edinburgh, a joyous and exuberant hi-tech tent, set against the powerful landscape of the crags, soars over a masonry plinth and amphitheater. The qualities of the land formations and the gothic town are given new dimension and vividness by the stunning juxtaposition of this contrasting insertion. This is contextualism without modesty, and Hopkins shows himself to be up to the task of creating a striking, monumental landmark without overwhelming a delicate setting.

In some of his smallest commissions, Hopkins shows that he has learned well the lessons of Cornell-style black plans, and he is able to make small buildings join with existing buildings to create beautifully composed new sequences of public space. At the Sheltered Housing, Charterhouse in London, two small Hopkins buildings join two 1820s gothic revival buildings to make a serene and beautiful new courtyard. The placement of his oval Queen's Building at Emmanuel College is so adroit that three old existing buildings that had no particular relationship to one another are now part of a series of beautifully framed vistas and handsomely composed spaces around the new building. This subtle, masterful game of urban composition, played with only one card, would make Colin Rowe stand and cheer.

Interestingly, Hopkins's weakest and least distinctive building is his venture into housing. This remarkably versatile and accomplished architect seems not to have found the means to cope with the Grand Inquisitors, even in their meeker British incarnations. His Jewish Care elderly housing project has a few nifty details, but it is basically an uninspired brick box wrapped around a not-so-beautiful courtyard. In this modest

Queens Building, Emmanuel College

commission, Hopkins is trapped by his own integrity. When the Grand Inquisitors do not allow him to manipulate tectonics and building methods through and through, he seems at a bit of a loss for what to do. Apparently, he cannot bring himself to articulate and give interest to building forms and materials that are just at the surface of ordinary and inexpressive building techniques. Obviously, he has the ability to do so; either it doesn't interest him, or he has a moral problem with manipulations of this sort.

Hopkins is really Hopkins when he has a decent budget, a complex program, and the challenge of a difficult context. The New Parliament Building seems to synthesize everything that has been evolving in his work for decades. It is in the most prominent and difficult setting one could imagine: facing the Thames with Big Ben and Pugin's incredible Palace of Westminster on one side, Norman Shaw's Queen Anne pile, New Scotland Yard, on the other, and the exuberant neo-baroque Foreign Office, all bristling with domes and turrets, just next door. It also sits directly on top of seven stories of the London Underground at Westminster Station, a condition that imposed structural problems of huge complexity.

Into this most demanding setting, Hopkins has inserted a monumental building of such lucidity that its every move seems ordained by some higher intelligence, like the stride of a leopard. He addresses a scenographic problem with technical means, creating a silhouette to blend with Shaw's chimneys, Pugin's gothic pinnacles, and the Baroque domes of the Foreign Office out of his own innovative ducts and stacks that are the latest word in low-energy passive air handling.

His predilection to erase the boundaries between inventive new technologies and ancient ways of building is perhaps best exemplified by his brilliant use of *post-tensioned* load-bearing masonry. The columns of the Parliament Building are made of sandstone. These slender, five-story columns have small-diameter steel rods threaded through them, with fancy details that allow them to be cinched down under tremendous tension. This composite column behaves like a piece of high-tech, prestressed concrete, has all the sensual qualities of the beautifully mottled sandstone, and is through and through real, not a veneer masquerading as structure. The columns diminish in section at each floor as the loads lighten. Flanking each column is a pair of bronze alloy ducts that grow in girth with each floor's added dirty air as the columns diminish. This extraordinarily expressive way of building is expensive and definitely is not the stuff of normative building and city fabric, but the post-tensioned columns and all the other highly inventive details related to structure, air handling, lighting, and other aspects of the Parliament Building enabled Hopkins to build a monument that is different in intent, and different in its impact on the city, than virtually all other monuments built in the last fifty years. The Parliament Building is a monument that expresses new ideas about the city, about time, and about environment at the same time that it eloquently addresses ideas about technology.

With the triumphant success of the Parliament Building, fame has finally caught up with Hopkins, and he now has had some international commissions thrust upon him. When asked to do environmentally sensible buildings for the desert emirate of Dubai, his approach is the inverse of those international stars who export the personal stylistics of their last hit. The questions he asks are "How did they used to build, before they had energy to burn and all the technology of the West?" and "What are the for-

New Parliamentary Building, London

mal, spatial, and tectonic possibilities of these old and sensible ways of building translated into contemporary ways of making things?"

We must wait to see how this most rooted of architects makes the transition to globe-trotting star. It is inconceivable that his long, patient research on the tectonics of the arch, the beam, and the vault could be adapted to normative buildings and their budgets. It is also hard to imagine how Hopkins would build in the United States, particularly the parts of the United States that are subject to earthquakes, where codes and deeply entrenched building practices seem always to dictate an antitectonics of concealed frames and nonstructural cladding, as opposed to his rigorous expressions of real structure.

The splendors of Hopkins's best buildings and the apparent difficulty he has with modest ones drive home the point of the last essays. For normal buildings, not monuments, for all those square miles of city fabric where the rule of the Grand Inquisitors cannot be challenged, urbanism itself—the making and remaking of the spaces of the city—is the serious architect's only refuge, and black plans are his best tool. Tectonics are denied to him like the pleasures of the harem. Occasionally, he may be allowed to flirt with the dark-eyed houris—a bracket here, a hanging canopy there, maybe a bit of nicely detailed stone or wood now and then, but nothing like the full-blown tectonic orgy of the Parliament Building, not even in his dreams.

We town makers cannot hope to emulate all aspects of Hopkins's work, but there is much that we can learn from him. We can learn from his catholicity about time, his side-stepping of the style wars, his immunity to the pretentiousness of the "conceptual." We can learn from a density of detail that makes new buildings comfortable neighbors to historic buildings, and we can learn that many of his dense and beautiful details are really pragmatic solutions to air handling and daylight. We can be inspired by the dignity of buildings that simply play it straight and solve their problems of habitation, environment, construction, and urbanism without histrionics or inflections of the personal but with the force of a careful and quiet intelligence.

The greatness of Hopkins's buildings lies in the fact they provide desperately needed antidotes to the very things that have been poisoning the world for decades. His work is postmodern, not in the sense of that short-lived and mostly dreadful wave of historicist pictorialism that swept through the architectural world twenty-five years ago, but in a much more profound and lasting sense. With scholarship and inventiveness, he has harnessed the craft of building to redress the phenomenological deprivations that modernity and more particularly modernism have subjected us to. His buildings are like a checklist of the categories of "nearness" that have been assaulted by the cities and buildings of the last fifty years. He has built an aesthetic out of controlling the nuances of daylight, of providing fresh unconditioned air, of minimizing the use of energy, of reinforcing the particularities of places and the sentient qualities of material, of locating us in the continuity of history as opposed to severing our time from olden times. One finds each of these qualities on occasion in the work of others, but in no other body of new architecture with such clarity of purpose, consistency, and eloquence.

Plano

Stretching to the horizon on both sides of the North Dallas Toll Road as it races north from the center of Dallas is the immense landscape of Plano, Texas. In the dialect spoken in this part of the world, "Plano, Texas" is indistinguishable from "plain old Texas." In this sense, it is an aptly named place, because Plano is the typical condition of the North American Edge City as it exists everywhere but nowhere on a vaster, more relentless, and terrifying scale than in Texas. If you ask whatever happened to the propositions of town building, put forth with such zeal and optimism by the modernists fifty and seventy-five years ago, one answer is Plano. Here you have Frank Lloyd Wright's decentralization and embrace of the automobile conjoined with the separation of uses preached by CIAM. All the elements of town—housing, work, commerce, entertainment, municipal administration—are separated from one another in the now totally predictable mish-mash of malls, power centers, business parks, residential planned developments, and the rest. And following the *dictat* of Le Corbusier, buildings and streets do not even greet one another in passing, each boogeying to the drumbeat of some inner music, like a crowd in which everyone is plugged into a Walkman. And, of course, to get from anything in Plano to anything else in Plano, you drive. There is simply no other way to get there.

Unlike their propositions about town building, however, modernist ideas about buildings caught on only partway in Plano. Office buildings are recognizable as Modern Architecture, more or less—mostly made of mirror glass, sometimes wrapped around rectangular boxes, sometimes taking on inexplicably complex shapes. But everything else is something else. The restaurants along the highway, for instance, sit in huge parking lots and are simulacra of objects and places from long ago or far away: Tudor castles, pharaonic tombs, ships, zeppelins, the Land of Oz, everything you can imagine. The shopping malls and the housing are, for the most part, tamer versions of this same sort of thing. This is the brand of reality celebrated by certain French intellectuals that reaches its apotheosis in the newer casino/hotels of Las Vegas.

Nothing about this landscape, except its remarkable size, is unfamiliar to anyone who has spent time on the planet recently, although a time traveler who last saw the world before 1948 would be completely bewildered. In the midst of all this, however, are two utterly remarkable places, and all the more astonishing because of what they are in the midst of. They are legitimate contenders for the world's finest pieces of new urbanism (or New Urbanism, if you prefer the proper noun).

The Legacy Town Center, now in progress, and the place called Addison Circle, now mostly built, are not just fragments or hints of what things might be like if things were different. They are fully realized places that are beautiful and satisfying in many of the same ways as the historic centers of European towns. When one is in the centers of Strasbourg or Bologna, one accepts their qualities as the way of the world and somehow forgets about all of the tragic junk one had to pass through to get there. One has the same blissful forgetfulness of edge city horrors in these two places that are still under construction.

As town planning and as architecture, Legacy Town Center and Addison Circle reverse the order of things as it exists in the rest of Plano and the Township of Addison, which engulf them. In these new places, buildings are not simply cast afloat in a matrix of undifferentiated space. There are real streets with rows of trees, brick sidewalks, and people walking. The buildings line the streets as in any old city, such as Boston or Zurich, but not Plano, Texas. When buildings are not busy making streets, they define the edges of courtyards, passageways, and public squares that are similar in size, feel, and quality of detail to the great squares of Georgian London. But this is not ersatz London or ersatz anything else. The architecture is not a revival or evocation of any other time or place. It is solid,

Addison Circle, streetscape

simple, well-constructed stuff that is decidedly modern in feel and technique, even if it is not exactly canonical modern architecture.

The various uses—housing, retail, office, hotels, civic buildings, recreation, public transportation—are mixed with one another, as in a traditional town, and, unlike the rest of Plano, the language of the architecture does not shift along with the uses of buildings. Here, you don't see Mediterranean townhouses reflected in the mirror glass curtain walls of office buildings. Buildings for different purposes are built in the same solidly made vernacular, and housing and offices look fine right next to each other. One would not think of the hotel chain Doubletree Inn as one of the great patrons of American architecture, but the Legacy Town Center Doubletree by the Dallas firm HKS is just right—festive, dignified, grand, well made—and, most importantly, it gives shape to the main public square of the town.

Addison Circle, with its consistently handsome buildings and its beautiful network of public and semipublic spaces, so contrasts with the sprawl around it that it creates a peculiar anomaly. The top floors of the taller buildings have distant views, but this is one place in the world where view is not an amenity, because the last thing one wants to do in Addison Circle is see out. It is hard to say whether the real estate implications or the phenomenological implications of this condition are more odd. In San Francisco, New York, or Hong Kong, the real estate market pays rich rewards for dwellings and workplaces that clearly locate their inhabitants in the universe and let them know where they are and what they are part of. Not here.

Addison Circle and Legacy Town Center turn the well-established world of Plano upside down. This achievement represents the coming together of a large number of people with a common purpose in a whole range of different disciplines, including finance, municipal government, urban design, architecture, traffic engineering, construction, and marketing. It began with almost simultaneous epiphanies experienced by two people in the unlikely setting of the real estate company started by legendary Dallas Cowboy quarterback Roger Staubach. Robert Shaw, the big guy who played center and snapped the ball to Roger, read Jane Jacobs's *Death and Life of Great American Cities*. Then he read Christopher Alexander's *Timeless Way of Building* and *A Pattern Language*, and he gave the books to his buddy Art Lomenick, Staubach's investment and development whiz. Then the two of them started reading everything about urbanism they could find, including *Collage City*, and they knew that there had to be something they could spend their energies on other than building more suburban garden apartments around Dallas.

In 1989, Shaw left Staubach to form Memphis Development—Memphis as in Egypt, not Tennessee, with a pyramid on the business card, no less. Memphis was dedicated to making great places "like Back Bay, Carmel or Paris—places people visit," and Lomenick joined him full-time in 1993 when things really got going. Lomenick, who calls himself the "emotional leader," really directed the development of the Addison Circle project. He describes his methods of building esprit on his construction crews. He says that during his readings he discovered that during the Hellenic Golden Age in the fifth century B.C., Egyptian pyramids were already ancient antiquities and the subject of archeological research. The Athenians, in the course of their excavations at Memphis, uncovered an inscribed stone deep within the pyramid. When they deciphered the hieroglyphics, they discovered that the inscription proclaimed for eternity, "THE RED TEAM KICKED THE BLUE TEAM'S ASS." This punchline does not have nearly the same impact on the printed page that it has when delivered in booming *hoch-Texan*.

For Lomenick, the lesson was clear. The pyramids were not the kind of everyday construction projects that Egyptians were used to, and they were built by teams who competed with one another to do something extraordinary. Without doubt, the pyramid builders did a helluva job, as did their Athenian students, so Lomenick invested in colored jackets for his crews, with team names and logos. Teams even had their own masseuses and trainers to keep them mentally and physically prepared for the ferocity of each day's competition. All of the crew members had to be convinced that this new way of working had messianic dimensions to it and that what they were part of was a big deal, both for them and for the people who would ultimately live in what they were building.

Lomenick's Addison Circle organization consisted of three separate development teams for the different neighborhoods, and three design firms with twelve different design principals participating. The lead urban designer was Paris Rutherford of RTKL in Dallas, with various other RTKL designers providing just the right degree of homogeneity and variation in the architecture.

The questions one asks over and over while strolling through these two remarkable places are, how on earth did they happen, why here of all places and, most importantly, is this a unique circumstance, or could new places of this quality and urbanity be built elsewhere? This last is the crucial question. It is as important and puzzling as the question of whether there is intelligent extraterrestrial life in the universe. In the long run, a lot depends on the answer.

Addison Circle and Legacy Town Center are remarkable achievements and hopeful signs, but they do not mean that the war is nearly over or that the juggernaut that produced the rest of the horrific landscape of Plano will be disarmed anytime soon. We are not so naive, because one thing that that was crushed forever in the collapse of modernism was the Enlightenment idea of progress. No one who cares about the quality of the world should dare to think that a few hopeful signs mean that things will soon be easier or that we are now all marching down the road to collective redemption together. The great revolution in the quality and nutritiousness of American cuisine has also produced the counterrevolution of Spam revival and chains like Johnny Rocket's, where people absolutely delight in stuffing themselves with the greasiest, fattest, sweetest, most synthetic concoctions ever purveyed as foodstuffs. Alice Waters has not prevented the obesity of teenagers from becoming as epidemic as the obesity of automobiles.

On that score, one might have thought that the market hegemony of lightweight, relatively nimble, economical cars a couple of decades ago would have settled the matter once and for all. Not so. One of the truly memorable news photographs of the year 2002 will be that of Senators John Kerry and John McCain slumped in their chairs, in postures of utter dismay and defeat, after their CAFÉ bill to increase the fuel efficiency of American cars lost 68 to 32 in the Senate. The sensibility of the bacon cheeseburger, the Lincoln Navigator (Pat Buchanan's favorite car), and the townscape of Plano is alive—and ready and eager to gobble us all.

One cannot draw conclusions from the fate or current condition of one individual, but the ups and downs of Lomenick's mercurial career may be a portent of some sort. The epiphany that he and Robert Shaw shared through their readings a little more than a decade ago led to what they both refer to as a guerilla movement, or Phase I of the revolution they helped to foment. That was the founding of Memphis Realty and the start of Dallas Uptown, the project that was the forerunner to Addison Circle and Legacy Town Center.

When Robert Shaw set his sights on the Uptown Neighborhood of Dallas in 1989, it was a derelict part of town, near downtown, with about three hundred residents scattered through two hundred acres of shabby buildings, vacant lots, and parking lots. Lomenick says that people rarely went out at night, because after dark the streets were ruled by packs of wild dogs. When he tells the story, it is accompanied by a convincing bared-fang, wild dog impersonation, just to make sure the point is clear.

There were no American sources of capital in 1989 with the slightest interest in Shaw's prescient vision of what Uptown has subsequently become—Dallas's swingingest neighborhood, and home to ten thousand new city dwellers. The remaining old buildings have been rehabilitated, there are hundreds of new residential and retail buildings, most of them handsomely designed, and there are streets with as much life as in any vibrant urban neighborhood in the country. Memphis was a shoestring operation that began its work with scrounged-together bits of overseas investment, and not much disclosure of what they were really up to.

The early successes of Uptown launched Phase II of their operation: Wall Street's first large-scale experiments with New Urbanism. When Lomenick joined Shaw in 1993, they formed the Columbus Realty Trust, a publicly traded company that gave them the capital to accelerate the growth of Uptown and begin half a dozen new projects, Addison Circle among them. The phone number for Columbus was 850-1492, a signifier that this operation had set about exploring a new world. Shaw and Lomenick had blind faith that this new world was not flat and that they would not fall off the edge of it.

Soon they discovered that more projects meant more staff, the need for even more capital, and a spiraling frenzy of commitments and growth. In 1997, Columbus merged with Post Properties, a publicly traded development powerhouse based in Atlanta. The completion of Addison Circle and Legacy Town Center are the products of Shaw and Lomenick's collaboration with John Williams, the dynamic CEO of Post, who was totally sympathetic to their intentions and means.

It was all going swimmingly, except for a fundamental flaw in the scheme. The demands placed upon Real Estate Investment Trusts by Wall Street investors put this New Urbanist wing of Post Properties into the same treadmill of relentless expansion that drives the fast-food industry. It is not the financial performance of individual projects that determines the rate of return on investment, but the rate of expansion of the company. Real Estate Investment Trust's (REIT's) calculations of their Funds from Operations (FFOs) are based on the *quarterly* growth of the fund.

Soon, the New Urbanist group within Post found themselves managing simultaneous projects in Austin, Phoenix, Los Angeles, Tampa, Orlando, Atlanta, Washington, D.C., Charlotte, Nashville, and New York. They were caught in an ever-accelerating centrifuge that did not support two things essential to the enterprise. First, a project like Addison Circle cannot be produced in the mindless frenzy that builds the simple formulaic real estate investments more familiar to Wall Street—the power centers, business parks, and residential planned developments that constitute the rest of Plano's landscape. Lomenick's team jackets, trainers, and masseuses are part of a patient remaking of the entire culture of American development and construction, from investment bankers to sheetrockers. The cheerleading, education, and inculcations of pride that Lomenick is so gifted at are the heart of the operation. They are indispensable to the quality of what is built—and they take time, more time than the impatient demands of capital floating around in a competitive capital marketplace can tolerate.

The second untenable characteristic of the centrifuge was what life on the centrifuge was like. John Williams is a wealthy man, a cultivated man, and not a young man. The ever-quickening pace of an ever-expanding empire lost its appeal for him, and in late 2000 he pulled Post out of its nationwide commitment to large, mixed-use New Urbanist communities. He is still actively working in Atlanta, but no longer in ten new cities all at the same time. Post's departure sent a ripple of gloom through many people who admired what they had done and considered it a major turning point.

Shaw had left Post in 1998 to start a similarly oriented company called Amico Partners, and Lomenick was temporarily left without a venue. An irrepressible soul, however, he never stopped pointing out some irrefutable fundamentals. Uptown, Addison Circle, and the other Columbus/Post projects are wildly popular, relatively immune to recession, deeply sound long-term investments, and serve the environmental agendas that increasingly control development entitlements. He has said this often enough and convincingly enough that very big players have listened to him. As of this writing, he has a new title as managing director for the Trammell Crow Company, Dallas's biggest and one of the nation's most important development organizations. In his person, New Urbanism now has a very good seat at what may be the best table in the house. So begins Phase III.

Over the long haul, despair is no more appropriate a response to transitory events than wild optimism is to the sight of Addison Circle. It is foolish to engage in a struggle to change things without a realistic assessment of what one is up against. Williams, Shaw, and Lomenick are highly resourceful, resilient people who have deep commitments to what they have been building, and they are not about to quit. More than anyone, *they* know that they are locked in a battle, a crucially important battle, for the quality of daily life. There is no end of the battle in sight; in fact, no end is conceivable. But there are two heartening things about these men. First, like zealots of all sorts, like Alice Waters and Julia Child, they are indefatigable. Second is that they *breed.* Amico Partners is just one of the new ventures started by Columbus and Post alumni. Even more significant is that many, many people see Addison Circle and they say with absolute resolve and conviction, "I want to do something as good as that."

Me too.

Epilogue

Humans are clever creatures, so clever at making things that they change their own circumstance from time to time: from hunter-gatherers to farmers, from cave dwellers to city dwellers. Their senses are keen, and they observe their planet closely—its seasons, its weather, its particulars of geography. They are also social creatures, who create complex organizations and communities to act in common, although they also can be unruly, cruel, and viciously competitive. It is partially to deal with these nasty characteristics of their own kind that they have made such complex societies.

After inhabiting their planet for a long time, they began to multiply in great numbers. They invented more and more tools, and in the most recent small fragment of their history, just the last five or six hundred years, they have swarmed over large areas of their planet. As they have done this, they have crowded together, made more and more complex tools, and made situations for themselves that many of them find novel and unfamiliar. They have made places where they cannot consort with one another as they need to, places where it is hard to tell where they are or what time it is, where their sharp senses go all awry. Some of them become unhappy or unhealthy. Some die prematurely.

Usually, after a time, their instincts and intelligence prevail, and they find ways to make their habitat congenial again. But their compulsive inventiveness and sheer numbers always are a threat to their own well-being and survival. Time and again, they set things right and then get them all messed up again.

It is human nature to invent and make things; that is why they are a successful species. They suffer debilitating frustrations when they can't just do what needs doing or build what needs building. Yet, through their very inventiveness, they keep erecting obstacles for themselves that make the simple act of making things more and more complex and indirect. It is profoundly unhealthy for them.

The things they make constantly change the world they live within. Because they have the power to alter the world much more rapidly than their own genetic makeup can adapt to, they are an anomaly in the whole scheme of natural selection and evolution. Other creatures flourish when their environment supports the way they are, or they die out when it does not. Humans, on the other hand, are consigned by their very nature to continually alter their habitat, but they must constantly struggle to make changes that are a reasonable match to their unchanging genetic appetites. It is a very complicated proposition.

For individual humans caught in a bad episode, it is no consolation that the species tends to set itself right after a time. One could not expect a Jew living in Krakow in 1940 to take a long view of things. The Third Reich lasted only twelve years, but that did not save him or his children.

Humans have an obligation that is unique among creatures—that is, constantly to evaluate their own inventions and social relations to keep them somewhere close to their own genetic needs. To do this, they need to know what it is they need, and there have always been whole classes of humans devoted to this study: shamans, priests, poets, artists. These people have an essential role for others—that is, to anchor them in the world and in the cosmos, to give them understanding of where they are in the continuity of time, in their communities with others, in the sanctuary of their own dwellings. This sense of being anchored in the world is a both a fundamental need for humans and a basic right. Simply keeping track of where we are has become so complex and urgent that some new kinds of philosophers and scientists have also taken up the task.

However, all of these wise people can't remake the world and keep it right for the others by themselves. They need architects and planners and builders—people who are the actual makers of the world. The people who design physical places need to be executors of the wisdom of the shamans, just as carpenters and masons are the executors of what it is that architects decide to build. This making of places for humans is important work because what they live in matters so very much to the health, the happiness, and the well-being of each one of these fragile, complex, and most amazing of all creatures.

BIBLIOGRAPHY

Alpert, Hollis. *Fellini: A Life*, 1st ed. New York: Marlowe, 1988.

Bacon, Mardges. *Le Corbusier in America: Travels in the Land of the Timid*. Cambridge: MIT Press, 2001.

Banham, Reyner. *Theory and Design in the First Machine Age*. New York: Praeger, 1960.

Blau, Eve. *The Architecture of Red Vienna, 1919–1934*. Cambridge: MIT Press, 1999.

Calthorpe, Peter. *The Regional City: New Urbanism and the End of Sprawl*. Washington, D.C.: Island Press, 2000.

Davis, Mike. *City of Quartz*. New York: Verso, 1990.

Dennis, Michael. *Court and Garden: From the French Hotel to the City of Modern Architecture*. Cambridge: MIT Press, 1988.

Frampton, Kenneth. *Modern Architecture: A Critical History*. New York: Oxford University Press, 1980.

———. *Modern Architecture and the Critical Present*. New York: Architectural Design Profile, 1982.

———. *Studies in Tectonic Culture: The Poetics of Construction in the Nineteenth and Twentieth Century Architecture*. Cambridge: MIT Press, 1995.

Garreau, Joel. *Edge City: Life on the New Frontier*. New York: Doubleday, 1991.

Giedion, Sigfried. *Space, Time and Architecture: The Growth of a New Tradition*. Cambridge: Harvard University Press, 1959

Gropius, Walter. *Scope of Total Architecture*. New York: F. W. Dodge, 1955.

Heidegger, Martin. "The Turning." *In The Question Concerning Technology and Other Essays*, pg 49. New York: Harper Torch Books, 1977.

Heidegger, Martin, and David Krell. *Basic Writings*. Vol. 1. New York: HarperCollins, 1976.

Heidegger, Martin, and Joan Stambaugh. *Being and Time: A Translation of Sein und Zeit*. SUNY Series in Contemporary Continental Philosophy. Albany: State University of New York Press, 1996.

Hitchcock, Henry-Russell, and Phillip Johnson. *The International Style*. New York: Norton, 1966.

Jacobs, Jane. *The Death of Great American Cities*. New York: Vintage Books, 1961.

———. *The Economy of Cities*. New York: Random House, 1970.

———. *Cities and the Wealth of Nations: Principles of Economic Life*. New York: Random House, 1984.

Koolhaas, Rem, and Bruce Mau. *S,M,L,XL: O.M.A.* New York: Monacelli Press, 1995.

Kostof, Spiro. *The City Shaped: Urban Patterns and Meanings through History*. London: Bulfinch, 1991.

Le Corbusier. *The Athens Charter*. New York: Grossman, 1973.

———. *Towards a New Architecture*. New York: Praeger, 1974.

———. *When the Cathedrals Were White*. New York: McGraw-Hill, 1964.

Lipsky, Florence. *San Francisco: The Grid Meets the Hills*. Marseille: Editions Parentheses, 1999.

Lynch, Kevin. *The Image of the City*. Cambridge: MIT Press, 1960.

Moudon, Anne Vernez. *Built for Change: Neighborhood Architecture in San Francisco*. Cambridge: MIT Press, 1986.

Mumford, Lewis. *The City in History: Its Origin, Its Transformations, and Its Prospects*. New York: Harcourt Trade, 1961.

Newbrun, Eva, and H. Peter Oberlander. *Houser: The Life and Work of Catherine Bauer*. Vancouver: University of British Columbia Press, 1999.

Norberg-Schulz, Christian. *Genius Loci: Towards a Phenomenology of Architecture*. New York: Rizzoli International, 1988.

Pevsner, Nikolaus. *An Outline of European Architecture*. London: Penguin, 1943.

Polt, Richard. *Heidegger: An Introduction*. Ithaca, New York: Cornell University Press, 1999.

Reps, John W. *The Making of Urban America: A History of City Planning in the United States*. Princeton: Princeton University Press, 1965.

Rowe, Colin. *As I Was Saying: Recollections and Miscellaneous Essays*. Vol 1. Cambridge: MIT Press, 1996.

Rowe, Colin, and Fred Koetter. *Collage City*. Cambridge: MIT Press, 1978.

Sennett, Richard. *The Conscience of the Eye: The Design and Social Life of Cities*. New York: W.W. Norton, 1990.

Smithson, Allison. *Team 10 Primer*. Cambridge: MIT Press, 1974.

Stimmann, Hans. *Berlin*. Hamburg: Gingko, 2000.

Wolfe, Tom. *Radical Chic and Mau-Mauing the Flak Catchers*. New York: Farrar, Straus and Giroux, 1970.

Wu, Liangyong. *Rehabilitating the Old City of Beijing: A Project in the Ju'er Neighborhood*. Vancouver: University of British Columbia Press, 1999.

Zimmerman, Michael E. *Heidegger's Confrontation with Modernity: Technology, Politics, and Art*. Bloomington: Indiana University Press, 1990.

INDEX